"Instacart for CMO's is a must read for anyone whose products are listed on Instacart. The book is full of clear, clean, well-written, and actionable advice. Kiri Masters is a true expert on retail marketplaces and knows exactly what it takes to win."

> — JASON "RETAILGEEK" GOLDBERG, CHIEF COMMERCE STRATEGY OFFICER, PUBLICIS

"Kiri is an eCommerce powerhouse. Instacart for CMOs will help you succeed not just on Instacart, but on any marketplace out there!"

> — RICK WATSON, CEO AND FOUNDER, RMW COMMERCE

"If Wikipedia and Babbel fell in love while shopping online for groceries, Instacart for CMOs would be their brainchild. Kiri Masters and Stefan Jordev have masterfully translated Instacart and this new class of omnichannel leader into a definitive go-to guide empowering commercial decision makers across CPG to navigate the next age of retail."

> — CHRIS PERRY, COFOUNDER, FIRSTMOVR

INSTACART FOR CMOS

HOW RETAIL BRANDS CAN HARNESS THE RAPID GROWTH OF INSTACART

STEFAN JORDEV

KIRI MASTERS

In the long, dark, early days of the COVID-19 pandemic, a star began to shine very brightly. That star had been there for a while, and most people knew its name. The star was orange and in the shape of a carrot, and it started pulling millions more customers into its orbit, followed by multi-billion dollar companies.

That carrot-shaped star — Instacart — is different to the marketplaces that have come before it. It is a four-sided marketplace (with consumers, in-store shoppers, retailers, and advertisers, explained in detail in Chapter 1) rather than a typical two-sided marketplace (with a consumer and a seller who may also advertise). It both solves a problem and creates a new problem for traditional retailers, in that Instacart is now an intermediary between the retailer and the end customer. And for branded manufacturers, while its advertising platform offers terrific return on investment, there are limits on how much control they have over their brand presence.

Why we wrote this book

We wrote this book because of the tremendous interest in Instacart as a marketing channel for brands, and the dearth of quality information for executives and hands-on-keyboard ecommerce practitioners alike on how to harness the power of the platform.

Ecommerce marketing software provider MikMak saw Instacart's adoption amongst its client base of mass-market consumer brands grow by 1900% in 2020. Instacart became MikMak's #4 trafficked retailer in 2020, behind Amazon, Target, and Walmart.

We saw a similar trend as practitioners of ecommerce marketplace growth solutions for brands at Bobsled Marketing: a huge spike in interest from brands who sought to harness the rapid volume shift of traditional grocery shopping dollars over to Instacart.

But there was very little "how-to" information about Instacart's marketing solutions, let alone strategic frameworks and best practices for brands. Inspired by the positive industry response to Kiri's 2019 book *Amazon for CMOs* (co-authored with Mark Power), which was recently ranked in the top 95 retail books of all time,[1] we set out to launch a book that lays out the strategic imperative for Instacart, a suggested playbook, and future opportunities.

Why listen to us?

Kiri launched the agency Bobsled Marketing in 2015, initially focused on providing managed services to branded manufacturers on Amazon across operations, brand protection, advertising, and organic marketing functions. Today

Bobsled is a fully remote team of 35 experts that established consumer brands rely on to grow and manage not only their Amazon sales channel, but Walmart and Instacart too. Kiri is the author of the books *Amazon for CMOs* (2019, co-authored with Mark Power), and *The Amazon Expansion Plan* (2017). Kiri has written a regular column for *Forbes* about Amazon and online marketplaces since 2018, and is the host of the Ecommerce Braintrust podcast.

Stefan Jordev is the Director of Marketplace Strategy and Insights at Bobsled Marketing. With over a decade of experience in performance marketing, Stefan played a key role in building Bobsled's industry-leading advertising capabilities on Amazon, Walmart and Instacart — leading the team that is now responsible for executing performance marketing campaigns for Bobsled's 70 clients. Stefan is a contributor to *BeautyMatter* and is frequently quoted as an advertising subject matter expert in publications like *Business Insider*, *Glossy* and *Modern Retail*.

In mid-2020 we began experimenting on the Instacart platform in order to become a resource and solution for brands who wanted to skip the learning curve and scale up quickly on Instacart. You'll hear from one of those clients later in the book. Bobsled also has an agency relationship with Instacart, which allows us to learn first-hand about new developments and opportunities on the platform, and best practices for implementing advertising solutions. However, we will point out that the contents of this book are our opinions, and the opinions of others who contributed their own insights, as cited individually throughout. This book is not authorized by Instacart, nor does Instacart sponsor the contents of this book.

In addition to our own experience, we have sought out the perspectives of executives from brands, solution providers, and retail thought leaders in order to provide a well-rounded account of the opportunities and existing limitations of the platform.

Our view

We believe that coming early to the party on Instacart is an enormous opportunity for many brands. The return on investment is exceptionally strong, and there's great value especially for replenishable items. Instacart's current and likely future capabilities point to it becoming a significant player in the retail media landscape, eventually challenging Amazon's market share.

But Instacart cannot be managed like other marketplaces. Due to structural differences, like Instacart's four-sided marketplace model and the codependency between Instacart and retailers, branded manufacturers face a new paradigm when it comes to accounting for Instacart's impact on their P&L and assigning internal ownership of the platform.

What you'll get out of the book

This book is designed to empower decision-makers to approach this critical moment confidently. We share insights into the most effective strategies and frameworks from the brands that we've worked with directly, and the retail leaders and practitioners that we interviewed specifically for the purpose of writing this book.

You can expect to learn from your peers about what successes they have seen so far, best practices, frameworks that have been tested, and thought experiments to consider before designing and refining your own company's strategy.

Our aim is that you finish reading this book confident that you understand the "full picture" of Instacart and the unique relationship it has with the end customer, your brand, and retail partners. We hope you feel encouraged by the exciting growth opportunities that your peers have already experienced. And most of all, we hope you use this knowledge and confidence to make bold decisions within your company and help move the industry forward.

Unfortunately for us, much of the content is likely to be outdated in less than a year; fortunately for you, it includes all of what we currently know as first-hand practitioners and from our interviews with over a dozen brands and retail industry thought leaders. If anything, it should provide you with a huge head start on a platform that does not yet command volumes of best practices and guidelines (like Amazon).

But we won't just look at the current state of play. We'll also consider where the players (brands, retailers, Instacart itself) are heading in the context of the entire ecommerce industry. We'll consider what Instacart's next moves might be, and how might they affect your brand. As a private company in an incredibly dynamic industry, there is plenty of space to speculate.

Let's get into it; there's no time to waste.

PART 1
PART I: WHAT IS INSTACART?

INSTACART FOUNDER APOORVA MEHTA was working for
Amazon when he came up with the idea for Instacart.
Mehta launched Instacart, a grocery delivery and pick-up
service, in San Francisco, with zero marketing or PR in
2012.

Within a year, it was being used by 1.5% of San Francisco
households.[1] Instacart provided a unique value proposition
to consumers: order items from your favorite grocery stores
conveniently from your phone, and have it delivered to you
within a couple of hours. No roaming the aisles, no queuing
in a checkout line, and no loading into and out of your car.

Instacart's first customers looked like many early adopters:
affluent consumers who would happily trade money for
time. A delivery fee of a few bucks and a slight markup on
the price of some items made far more sense than spending
two hours doing a grocery run.

. . .

Instacart attracted investment funding and continued its rollout through the US until 2017, when it hit what would be considered, at the time, a setback: Whole Foods, one of Instacart's most-shopped stores, delisted from the platform after Amazon purchased the grocer. But this was actually the beginning of big things for Instacart.

Karen Short, Managing Director at Barclays Investment Bank and author of the report *Dissecting the Instacart Addiction*, says that the first reaction for everybody in the industry was, 'Instacart is toast'. But instead Instacart became a lifesaver for many food retailers in the country, as shopping behaviors continued to change and Amazon appeared to be on the warpath to disrupt the grocery category. "The assumption that this whole acquisition would kill Instacart turned out to be categorically false, and in fact, the exact opposite happened. Instacart became the only solution for many retailers in the United States," said Short in an interview on the *Digital Grocer* podcast.[2]

Between 2017 and today, Instacart has also benefited from a global pandemic that has accelerated a shift to ecommerce by what some retail experts estimate to be five years.[3] Accordingly, there is a rush to capture the consumer demand on this burgeoning marketplace from brands and retailers alike.

. . .

Instacart is a 'four-sided' marketplace

Most other online marketplaces are two- or three-sided. Etsy sellers sell to Etsy buyers. Amazon customers purchase from Amazon sellers (third party sellers or 3P) about half the time, and from Amazon itself (via first party vendors or 1P, and from Amazon's own private label brands) the rest of the time.[4] But Instacart has four important stakeholders that interact with each other:

- The end customer, who places an order on Instacart.
- The in-store shoppers, who pick the customer's items and deliver to their door. Shoppers may interact with customers within the app, for example to advise of out-of-stock items and recommend replacement items.
- Advertisers, generally branded manufacturers who want to get their products in front of Instacart shoppers at the point of purchase.
- Retailers, who make their product assortment available on Instacart and allow the shoppers to pick, pack and deliver from their stores.

In this book we use Instacart's own terms for these stakeholders: "Shoppers" are the gig workers who pick, pack, and deliver an order. "Customers" are the end-users of the service. The main stakeholder we're addressing in this book is the advertisers or branded manufacturers, which we'll refer to as "Brands".

. . .

It is commonplace for a brand to refer to a retail partner as a "customer" but we will avoid doing so in this book to prevent confusion with end customers.

Due to the four-sided nature of its marketplace, Instacart operates differently to other online marketplaces like Amazon and Walmart. There are six key differences, which we'll expand on in this chapter before doing a direct comparison with other major marketplaces in the US.

1. Retailers rule the roost

The retailers are a key stakeholder that have a significant and unique role to play. They are the ones who are responsible for inventory availability, pricing, and product content. This is a unique situation in the world of online marketplaces, where the brand manufacturers usually control all of these elements.

As such, brands are placed in the unusual position of relying on their retail partners to be on top of their Instacart integration and implementation, simply to ensure that a brand's products will appear when a customer searches for them on the Instacart app.

2. Vast assortment

One of Instacart's key competitive advantages is that by inking an agreement with a single retailer, it can add hundreds of thousands of new SKUs to its assortment. This was particularly pertinent in 2020 as Instacart began expanding aggressively outside of its core grocery category. Assortment is a key competitive advantage for a market-place since selection (along with competitive pricing) attracts customers, and beauty, pharmacy, and liquor are all categories that can now be shopped on Instacart. Once customers have shopped with Instacart in one category and developed trust with the service, they are likely to use the platform to shop another category.

3. Instacart is a media platform

A key point we'll expand on later in this book is that brands should view Instacart as a media platform. As Chris Cantino, the co-founder of CPG brand Schmidt's Naturals (sold to Unilever in 2017) and co-founder of Color VC, says, "Instacart is a demand aggregator."

Due to the full lifecycle of shopping behavior occurring on Instacart (research, browsing, transacting, and repurchas-ing), brands can use Instacart as another platform to reach customers at each stage of their buying journey: building brand and product awareness, and driving direct-response actions.As such, brands should view Instacart as a media platform like Facebook or Google, rather than a distribution channel over which they have limited control.

4. Instacart struggles to find a 'home' within brands

Sales from Instacart show up on a brand's P&L within their retailer Purchase Orders (POs),

and Instacart does not provide sales data at the retailer level. This makes it hard for brands to understand the impact that Instacart has on their topline revenue numbers.

To add more complexity, media spend on Instacart is often attributed to the ecommerce or digital advertising budget, which doesn't get credit for incremental POs from retailers.

We discuss this conundrum further in Chapter 8, 'Instacart's strange relationship with a brand's org chart and P&L', as well as how some brands are approaching it.

5. First-mover advantage

All of the brands we spoke with have concluded that their investment on Instacart is paying significant dividends. With Instacart's self-serve advertising platform which launched in May 2020, it's a new platform with low competition. Compared with a more established marketplace advertising platform like Amazon Advertising, Instacart's return on advertising spend (ROAS) is very high. We discuss Instacart advertising in detail in Chapter 7.

. . .

Another advantage of being early to the party is that replenishable products benefit handily from a user experience that heavily promotes prior purchases. Getting into a customer's cart now could pay real dividends in years to come.

6. Order fulfilment

A key distinction between Instacart and the other online grocery platforms is Instacart's relationship with Inventory and Order Fulfillment. With Instacart, this is completely operated by the retailer. This greatly simplifies Instacart's business model: no additional inventory or order management is required, freeing up huge amounts of working capital that its competitors spend on inventory and warehousing. Instacart can divert its capital expenditure toward maturing its systems — its advertising platform in particular.

The downside, however, is for brands, who cannot control product availability. Instead, the retailers control availability, and many retailers are lagging behind with their own ordering systems and visibility into inventory positions. The implications for brands include:

- Launching a new product or brand can be difficult. New products will only be available on Instacart once a retailer has it in stock. This is where it's important to have a close relationship with retailers and to educate them on your expectations for the product and the accompanying marketing plan.

- Some products won't be available in certain regions, if local retailers aren't stocking that product. This means that the product won't show in organic search results and the brand won't be able to run Featured Product ads for that product in those regions.
- If a retailer's ability to monitor its inventory at the store level is poor, it creates bad outcomes for the customer and for the brand. The brand might be running advertising on a product that is actually out of stock in that zip code, the customer is frustrated when the product isn't available, and the shopper might suggest a competing product that is available in-store.

	Inventory Relationship	Paid search Advertising	Shopper Frequency* (last 30 days)	Organic Optimization	Order Fulfilment
amazon	1P or 3P	Robust, but complex, competitive	53%	Extensive options, great ROI	Amazon fulfilment is best practice
Walmart	1P or 3P	Limited, expensive	44%	Limited, good ROI	Merchant fulfils is best practice
TARGET	1P or 3P (invite-only)	Limited	22%	Limited	3P: Merchant Fulfils 1P: Target fulfils from store
instacart	None	Limited, but great ROI	15%	Limited	Retailer fulfils
Kroger	1P or 3P (new)	Limited	13%	Limited	Merchant fulfils

Above: a visual comparison of Instacart vs other grocery marketplaces[1]

Another distinction between Instacart and Amazon is an element of competition with national brands. Amazon commands a "frenemy" status for many brands who had a successful presence on the platform, only to wake up to find Amazon launching competing private-label products. This was a major issue that the US Congress raised in its antitrust hearings in 2020. As Kiri wrote for *Forbes*, Amazon has two key advantages: it generates a huge volume of fees from brands, and it also develops its own products based on what's working for those same brands.[2] Walmart, Target, Kroger, and other retailers also have thriving private label brands. But the same cannot be said for Instacart — it has no private label products and is agnostic as to which brand or product wins the sale.

PART 2

PART II: WHY YOUR COMPANY SHOULD CARE ABOUT INSTACART

To GET a sense of how Instacart was making inroads in the Canadian market, Kiri asked a Winnipeg-based Bobsled Marketing employee if they had shopped on Instacart lately, and what grocery delivery services their family was currently using. Although the answer at the time was "none", it eventually prompted that employee to introduce the Instacart app to her Boomer-generation mother. An order arrived from a regional butcher store within 45 minutes of placing it, delivered by a friendly shopper — a truly delightful experience. The employee heard her mother raving about Instacart to her husband for the next 30 minutes, and subsequently over the phone with her sisters and half a dozen friends in the area. It's safe to say that many more Instacart orders will be placed in Winnipeg in the coming months.

This is a vignette of the rise of Instacart: a solution that is so good that it's worth raving about. In this chapter we'll look at how Instacart has captured the market.

. . .

Instacart today

While Instacart has expanded into non-grocery cate-gories, grocery is still currently the bulk of their business and represents the segment with the greatest in-home delivery challenges to date (i.e. harder for the retailers to execute themselves).

Grocery has historically been one of the most challenging retail categories to migrate into an online environment, due to the product assortment often being heavy, bulky, or perishable. Compounding the logistical challenges, ecom-merce as a channel is generally one of the least profitable avenues for these brands to sell through. As a result, devel-oping an online marketing and distribution capability has been fairly low on the priority list for these brands.

However, 2020 changed the way we live, shop, and work, bringing both challenges and opportunities for brands and companies.

Instacart has been around since June 2012, but demand exploded during the COVID-19 pandemic lockdowns. Homebound consumers came to rely on in-home delivery in numbers that had never been seen before. Instacart jumped at the opportunity and boosted its capacity to service customers:

- Increased the number of shoppers by 3X
- Increased the number of care agents by 15X
- Added 150+ new partners, 1,500+ pickup locations and 10,000+ new stores[1]

With consistent investment in such expansion efforts, Instacart is now available to 85% of US households and 70% of Canadian households.

By rapidly expanding capacity and rising up to meet newfound demand, Instacart pulled ahead of competitors in the online grocery race. According to data from Second Measure, Walmart led market share among top delivery services before the pandemic, with share of sales consistently over 50%. But since March 2020, Instacart has emerged as the industry leader, eclipsing Walmart Grocery, and capturing 48% market share by June.[2]

The performance, expansion, and execution during COVID by Instacart is to be applauded, especially when comparing their growth to rivals Shipt and Peapod (who had a 23-year head start in grocery delivery).

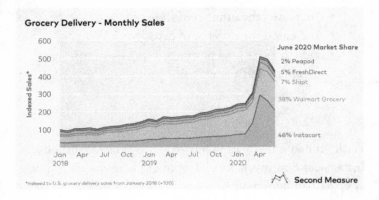

Above: Second Measure report showing Instacart's growth in monthly sales

This growth is what also drew branded manufacturers to initiate or accelerate relationships with Instacart. Snack brand Clif Bar & Company (CLIF BAR) initially struck up a relationship with the marketplace largely because both companies were based in the San Francisco Bay Area. Julie Liu, Shopper Marketing Manager at CLIF BAR, says: "When we started with them, we saw it as a way to help support regional grocery retailers that don't have built-up marketing capabilities to scale." Liu says their investment really accelerated in 2019 and even more so in 2020 when the pandemic created the ultimate business case for Instacart.

Instacart also took the opportunity to expand much further beyond the grocery category in 2020, announcing partnerships with Best Buy, Walmart, Staples, Bed Bath & Beyond, Buy Buy Baby, Sephora, and 7-11, among others.

Instacart boosts brick and mortar accounts

The use-case for investing on Instacart is different compared to other ecommerce platforms, because sales from Instacart ultimately show up with your brick and mortar retailer accounts. This certainly has the potential to cause conflict in your company's P&L, as explained in much greater detail in Chapter 8.

But investment in Instacart can also be used as a leverage point with your retail customers — proving that you're not just yanking advertising spend from their shopper marketing programs as the marketing spend is being used to drive sales through their stores. It's bittersweet for retailers — they won't be as happy as if you were spending those advertising dollars on end-caps and in-store promotions, but they will see those promotional efforts showing up as Instacart sales. We also cover the retailer perspective in greater detail in Chapter 10.

First-mover advantage

Instacart's current setup is one where in order to win years from now you need to win today. Investing in the platform early on — particularly though advertising investment — will allow your products to get ahead of the competition in a couple of ways. One of these is by capturing the 'badges' associated with top-selling products: "Store choice" and "Popular" were the two main badges available at time of writing. These badges improve Click Through Rates (CTR) and conversion rates well into the future.

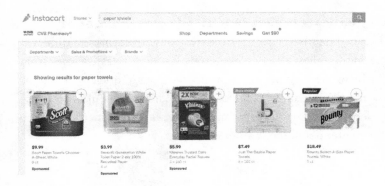

Above: Instacart's Featured Products, Store Choice, and Popular products

Another huge dividend that brands can expect to see from early investment in Instacart is through repurchasing activity. Once a particular product gets in an Instacart user's 'past purchases' basket, it is much easier to influence buyers towards a repeated purchase. Instacart also nudges its users to re-order items that have been added to their basket in the past.

In a webinar presentation to brand and agency advertisers in Q4 of 2020, Instacart said that 20-25% of shopping activity comes from repurchasing. This creates a constant validation loop of getting consumers to buy items that they already bought in the past which is, of course, incredibly beneficial for brands.

"I'm having conversations with CMOs across our brands to help them understand what's going on here. Right now there is a land grab going on for the first purchase of these initial consumers."

— John Denny, VP eCommerce & Digital Marketing at CAVU Ventures

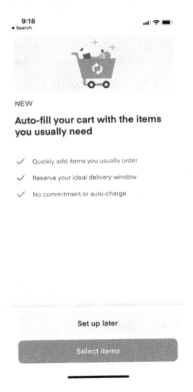

Above: Example of Instacart nudging a customer toward their past purchases, but encouraging them to "auto-fill your cart with the items you usually need"

Our view is that investing in Featured Product ads today offers benefits that expand beyond immediate ROI, and that a portion of a company's brand marketing budget should be dedicated towards it.

The Instacart team is more accessible

Most brands are happy with the relationship they have with Instacart, saying that the Instacart team is very responsive. This is praise that we don't often hear from brands about their relationship with Amazon or Walmart.

Instacart has hired a lot of employees from Amazon and Walmart, as well as advertising agencies like Edge By Ascential and Omnicom, paving the way for closer relationships with brands and agency partners.

Melissa Burdick, Co-founder and President of ad-tech solution Pacvue, applauds Instacart's ability to move quickly when launching new features. Pacvue was given the opportunity to be one of the first to start working with Instacart's new advertising API which launched in May of 2020. Pacvue started working with Instacart in May and was able to launch its Instacart advertising solution in June.

· · ·

From an agency perspective, we have found Instacart to be more accessible and ready for feedback than most other advertising platforms. But it's clear that Instacart is cautious about rolling out its advertising solution too quickly and providing a poor experience. When Instacart launched its self-serve advertising solution early in 2020, it only onboarded four ad-tech providers with direct access to its API: Pacvue, Kenshoo, Tinuiti and Flywheel.

Molly Dufner, VP Ecommerce and Customer Experience at e.l.f. Cosmetics says that the Instacart team has been very receptive to creative joint marketing ideas between the companies. But with the pandemic, it forced some of those outside-the-box ideas onto the backburner:

> "The willingness is there. It's just a matter of resources and priorities right now. Their business grew unexpectedly — what they thought might happen over five years happened in three months. But they're responding well to that. So the ideas and the willingness are there —there are more things to come and it's just a matter of timing."

BEFORE PROJECTING Instacart's growth into the future, it may be worth exploring the question about online grocery's growth in general. Data shows that online grocery will continue to grow in coming years. Online grocery will swell to 21.5% of total US grocery sales by 2025, more than doubling its share of the overall grocery market at the end of 2020.[1]

But will online grocery shopping become a relic of the COVID era, with consumers returning to in-store shopping once they are able to move around more freely? The ecommerce professionals that we spoke with for this project are unanimous that Instacart will continue to grow past the pandemic, driven by their user growth, and the convenience it offers to its users. And a study by BCG found that customers who shop online five times over a three-to-four month period are likely to stick to online long-term.

. . .

A study by BGC shows that 35% of US customers new to ecommerce in March plan to continue making grocery purchases online after COVID-19 restrictions are over. By 2022, ecommerce's share of individual grocery categories is expected to be as much as three times higher than pre-COVID-19 levels and two times higher than forecasts before the pandemic.[2]

Instacart customers are buying more on the platform, and the basket sizes are increasing. In a webinar presented to advertisers in November 2020, Instacart said that total order volume grew 500% and there was a 35% increase in average basket size in the first half of 2020.

> "Every piece of research I've seen shows that consumers who came over to the Instacart platform have continued buying more, and buying more often. In other words, these consumers are not going anywhere."

— Jim Morgan, Vita Coco.

In this chapter we'll look at the case for Instacart's continued growth, as well as potential setbacks and challenges that the company may face in future years.

History repeating itself

As Google was growing its search business in the 1990s, there were many websites that didn't want to drive traffic to or from Google as they wanted to build out their own search engine. But the adoption of Google by so many users created such a lock-in effect that those websites soon didn't have a choice — they had to rely on Google as a search engine.

As John Denny, VP Ecommerce and Digital Marketing at CAVU Ventures explains:

> "We saw with Google and media players, where the *New York Times* didn't want to default to Google as its source of traffic, but found that there was nothing they could do about it. Because Google as a source, and a preferred consumer platform, begins to create the momentum, that means there's nothing that you can do. And we see this in [other] digital environments."

We saw a similar play unfold with Amazon over the past 15 years. Amazon created demand with a value-priced assortment in specific categories, which attracted customers. Retailers like Toys 'R' Us saw the demand aggregation occurring on Amazon and decided to provide their assortment to Amazon. This further stoked selection for customers, increasing customer demand to the point where eventually brands themselves wanted to directly be part of the action. Amazon now accounts for half of ecommerce sales in the US.

. . .

History has a way of repeating itself and in this case, two-hour grocery delivery as the preferred shopping solution for many customers means that many brick and mortar retailers have no choice but to partner with Instacart — the most sophisticated solution of its kind available today. This creates a flywheel of sorts for Instacart: more retailers means a wider product assortment, which attracts more customers, which in term attracts more retailers and advertisers who want to capture that demand.

The business model of data

One important factor that paves the way for Instacart's future growth (and mirrors Google and Amazon's strategy) is the huge volume of data that they have acquired. The basket data they are getting from millions of customers will allow them to anticipate future demand and adjust to the market demands much faster than competitors, or even the individual retailers that they partner with.

The demand data and other behavioral data that Instacart now holds is extremely valuable to brands. Such data can be used to target customers at highly specific stages of the buying process, to lure customers away from competitors, to generate trial purchases, to expose customers to innovative new products, and to remind existing customers to repurchase. Shopper data can also be used to target customers based on household composition and interests.

Amazon is the third-largest advertising platform in the world, after Facebook and Google. The allure of Amazon advertising comes from its unique vantage point into the actual purchasing habits of hundreds of millions of customers — something that Facebook and Google simply can't replicate. Instacart holds a similar vantage point, and might just be able to give Amazon a run for its money. Advertising is a highly profitable revenue stream that Instacart is likely to invest in significantly over the coming years.

Andrew Lipsman of Insider Intelligence predicts that post-COVID, a "retail media trio" of Amazon, Walmart, and Instacart will rise up to challenge the Facebook-Google duopoly:

> "Retailers have a key advantage over Facebook and Google as media sellers. Their platforms are powered by the combination of high-intent keyword searches and shopper data, giving them an even better ability than their duopoly counterparts to target the right customers with ads." [3]

Amazon's assortment extends across most shopping categories, and it has built a deep understanding of particular categories (electronics for example). But the grocery category has been a harder nut to crack. Instacart's advantage is in developing insight into a retail category that Amazon has historically been weaker in and providing Instacart with a competitive view of the customer.

. . .

The strength of a marketplace is to buy more, sell more, learn more. In Instacart's case, they are focusing solely on the latter two factors. Instacart's ability to predict future demand means they can deploy resources more strategically, in areas such as improving staffing.

Instacart International?

One of Instacart's unique strengths is the scale of its retail partnerships. With more than 500 retailers onboard as of 2020, Instacart is the preferred delivery partner for retailers. This strength — the ability to onboard and maintain hundreds of retailer partnerships — could be leveraged in international markets.

Instacart already redefined a previously held expectation that online grocery will only be available for major cities.

"The expectation was that online grocery may cap out at what were then called the 'NFL cities' — the top 25 or 30 metro areas. Instacart showed that with the really asset-light business model and 1099 contractors, you don't need to pay benefits and you can expand even more broadly."

— Keith Anderson, SVP of Strategy & Insights at ecommerce analytics firm Profitero

The US makes up just 17% of the global grocery market, online and offline,[4] meaning that there is plenty of room for growth outside the US.

In fact, Instacart already has a small but growing foothold in the Canadian market. The service reaches more than 85% of households in the US and more than 70% in Canada.[5] The company's growth there indicates how quickly the asset-light, partner-driven model can scale: in November 2017, Instacart launched in Toronto and Vancouver with Loblaw as its sole partner. Within six months, Instacart had expanded to 11 Canadian markets, and in September 2018, Instacart added service from Walmart Canada stores, Staples Canada and M&M Food Market.

A potential growth area for Instacart is to take its technology and retail partner model into other established markets like the UK, Germany, Mexico, and Australia.

Potential setbacks and challenges to Instacart's growth

While Instacart certainly looks to be riding high in 2021, it's also worthwhile casting an eye to the future to consider some competitive threats that Instacart might face.

Threat 1: Retailers developing their own platforms

A potential challenge towards Instacart could be retailers developing their own home delivery platforms in the future. Retailers are critical to Instacart's success in its current model, since retailers are the sole source of all inventory and a substitute for Instacart building any of its own fulfillment centers.

> "I have always heard the sentiment from retailers — and even some suppliers — that Instacart is commonly viewed as a bridge strategy for players that currently don't have the scale, will or skill to go build their own capabilities."

— Keith Anderson, SVP of Strategy & Insights at ecommerce
analytics firm Profitero

By conceding control of the last mile to Instacart, retailers lose the ability to affect the user experience. This is arguably one of the most personal connections with end customers. As Instacart becomes that trusted entity that literally "delivers the goods" for consumers, where will the loyalty lie — with the retailer or Instacart?

It turns out that if a customer is loyal to a specific retailer (customer favorites like Wegmans, Costco, and Sprouts come to mind), they will not hesitate to switch from Instacart to that retailer's native app. This threat is discussed in detail in this book in Chapter 10 — 'The Retailer Connection'.

. . .

A related scenario is if a competitor starts scooping up exclusive retailer partnerships. DoorDash, Uber, and Shipt are the most likely candidates in this case. Associated Food Stores, a Salt Lake City-based cooperative of more than 400 stores, has to date used DoorDash for order delivery, since its commission rate was lower than Instacart's.[6]

On the other hand, last-mile delivery partners are most effective at expanding a retailer's (or brand's) reach. Restaurants and fast-food operators quickly realized that being loyal to a single platform like Uber Eats was not in their interest, as consumers tend to be loyal to a single app. Having multiple delivery partners could also facilitate more competition between providers and lower costs over time.

Threat 2: Too slow to win advertising share

As we discuss later in the book, national brands have begun adopting Instacart advertising with gusto. Instacart offers a unique way to target customers, and the platform is delivering a great return on ad spend. But in order to secure more of those lucrative advertising budgets, Instacart will need to up its game quickly. Brands need more levers to pull, aside from the self-serve Featured Product ads and limited promotion types. Especially if threat #1 comes to pass, Instacart will only have more competition fighting for advertising dollars in the future.

There has been a rush of retailers launching media platforms or seeking to grow existing platforms as a means to improve profitability. Instacart will be one of many places for brands to spend their advertising budget. The advantage that retailers have against Instacart is the ability to measure closed loop attribution. This means that brands can measure the success of their online activation both online and offline — a very compelling proposition for brands. Instacart's current model does not allow for this closed loop attribution.

Threat 3: Staying profitable

As of the time of writing, Instacart has had one profitable month, in April 2020.[7] While Instacart has been a privately funded company, it could choose to focus on consolidating market share and proving out its internal strategy. However, there has also been discussion of an IPO for Instacart. This would put pressure on Instacart to care about the factors that Wall Street cares about (like consistently returning profits to shareholders) and to deliver returns to shareholders — not necessarily the same things that Instacart would push on its own.

We also expect competition to heat up in the space. While Instacart has an early-mover advantage, expect competitors to offer lower commission rates, which will impact Instacart's ability to retain retail partners.

Threat 4: Instacart's 'gig' workforce

Most of Instacart's in-store shoppers are gig workers. Instacart has come under fire on various occasions for its treatment of these gig workers, and has faced various controversies around conditions and pay. State and federal governments around the world are putting a spotlight on the 'gig economy' and in which situations these workers would be entitled to employer benefits. Any big change to legislation in this area could negatively impact Instacart's business model.

Legislative action aside, new entrants are emerging that could challenge Instacart around retaining its workforce. Dumpling,[8] for example, provides professional shoppers with the resources to migrate off the Instacart platform and start their own personal-shopping business.

Threat 5: A return to "normal"

The popular belief among industry analysts is that online grocery will keep growing in a post-COVID world, or at least that online shopping will remain at elevated levels. But there is still a threat to Instacart if consumers return en-masse to physical stores and eating out at restaurants, rather than shopping and preparing food at home.

PART 3
PART III: WHAT INSTACART CHANNEL MANAGEMENT LOOKS LIKE

THE WORDS of advertising industry thought leader Tom Goodwin were immortalized in a post for Techcrunch in 2015 called *The Battle Is For The Customer Interface:*[1]

> "Uber, the world's largest taxi company, owns no vehicles. Facebook, the world's most popular media owner, creates no content. Alibaba, the most valuable retailer, has no inventory. And Airbnb, the world's largest accommodation provider, owns no real estate."

And Instacart is on track to win a new customer interface victory: "Instacart, the most valuable delivery app, owns no trucks or warehouses."

Such is the business model of Instacart — an unusual hybrid of last-mile fulfillment and front-end app, that relies on retail partners for inventory instead of holding its own. The unique combination of things that Instacart *is* and *isn't*, dictates the suitability of the platform for your business.

In this chapter we will analyze if investing in Instacart is right for your brand based on its unique operational model.

You can't choose to be on Instacart

Brands who are interested in building their presence on Instacart's platform are often surprised to learn that they can't just choose to be on Instacart. After all — the ability to sell on marketplaces like Amazon and Walmart is in the hands of the aspiring brand. Why not Instacart?

The only path to distributing products on Instacart is through their retailer partners. This is because Instacart holds no inventory themselves. Instead, retailers send data feeds with UPCs of products being sold in their stores to Instacart, who then make those products available for sale based on the zip code of the customer.

As such, brands can only use Instacart if they are being sold in one of Instacart's brick and mortar retail partners. So the question becomes how to use your influence as a brand to increase POs with your retail buyers.

"My advice [on how to get on Instacart] would be to really understand how you can influence your retail buyer," says

Julie Liu, Shopper Marketing Manager, Omnichannel at CLIF BAR. Liu says that there is not often a retail buyer who's dedicated to Instacart, and that the onus might be on the brand to educate the buyer about the growth you're seeing in online grocery, and Instacart's capabilities. It's a conversation that brands need to have with their buyers about the levers they each have available to drive sales.

Not just for grocery

In 2020, Instacart also expanded their retailer partners to include non-grocery channels like 7-Eleven, Staples, SEPHORA, Five Below, Disney and many others to provide even more value to consumers. This means that Instacart is no longer the sole domain of CPG brands. Early adopters in such categories as beauty, office supplies, and pharmacy items could benefit from an early lead in the 'race to convenience' if they make moves now.

One category that could particularly benefit from Instacart is liquor. Due to varying regulations in US states, liquor brands often have issues related to actual distribution and also advertising on Amazon and Walmart, but their access to US households is much easier with Instacart. Instacart told us at the time of writing that it has the largest alcohol delivery service in North America, with alcohol delivery available in 23 states plus Washington, DC via partnerships with more than 200 retail partners that sell liquor products.

Instacart does not hold a liquor license, but instead partners with retailers that are already licensed to sell alcohol. This makes it easy for brands to get started with a wide selection of Alcohol Enabled Retailers, including liquor stores and traditional grocery stores.[2]

> "One of the key benefits of Instacart is just the fact that it opens up this marketplace for alcohol brands to bid when they haven't been able to do that on Amazon or Walmart."

— Melissa Burdick, President and Co-Founder of Pacvue

Instacart's featured products are available for alcohol brands in California

How much brands are investing in Instacart

Relative to other marketplace channels, Instacart attracts a lower level of spend from most brands right now. Of the brands that we spoke with, most are spending significantly more of their advertising budget on Amazon. Melissa Burdick, Co-Founder and President of advertising technology company Pacvue, says that brands are generally still in testing mode with Instacart and using "leftover" ad budget form their other digital platforms like Amazon.

But it is traditional and in-store marketing spend that appears to have migrated to Instacart. When the pandemic hit, many brands — especially CPG brands — shifted their TV ad budget to Instacart and other digital channels.

The percentage of advertising investment into Instacart is still lower compared to other channels, with Amazon dominating still in terms of spend.

As we discuss more in Chapter 8, Instacart generally occupies two positions in most brands' P&Ls, making it harder for brands to justify where the advertising budget comes from, and exactly what it should be.

For our clients at Bobsled Marketing, we generally recommend 10% of their total advertising budget is spent on "experimental" channels and strategies. This could be used for a new video-ad format on Amazon, but it could also be used to begin working with Instacart as a new advertiser. (Once a channel or advertising strategy is proven, that ad spend is no longer considered experimental, and a brand should seek new opportunities to continue iterating and avoid standing still in a competitive environment.)

. . .

The main benefit of performance-driven marketing is its measurability against sales. With this in mind, brands will have a good idea of whether the new platform works for them relatively fast — in the case of Instacart, within a few months.

Promote the whole assortment or part of the assortment?

Because retailers, not brands, control inventory positions on Instacart, it's common to see a brand's whole assortment on Instacart. And that is certainly what many brands want to see.

But brands do get to choose which products to prioritize from an advertising standpoint. A brand can choose to advertise its top-performing products only — thus increasing their ROAS (return on advertising spend) and creating a flywheel effect for these products as they are suggested as repeat purchases in the future. Brands could also choose to promote newer products if they are entering a new market, or boost products that have not performed well organically.

Some brands that we spoke with said that while Instacart encourages brands to promote their entire assortment, they are choosing instead to focus on profitable 'hero' SKUs first. This is particularly true while Instacart has limited capability for brands to optimize product page content — many brands don't want to promote product pages that are under-optimized and less likely to convert.

. . .

At Bobsled Marketing we see a variety of strategies being employed by brands, depending on whether their goal is primarily profitability or growth. As a general rule of thumb, we recommend brands actively advertise the top-performing 20% of their assortment.

The power of instant gratification

Molly Dufner from e.l.f. says that Instacart's super-fast delivery capabilities is what drives their interest in the platform. In chapter 6 we'll go in more detail on how e.l.f. Cosmetics directs its customers to transact on Instacart or other channels, depending on the customer's preference.

"As a brand, we're still looking for these ways of providing instant satisfaction to our customers. We have the largest direct ecommerce business in the US mass-beauty market. So we have all these great customers, we have a loyalty program, and we want to be able to give them new and innovative ways that they can get our products."

While Amazon and Walmart have various programs that offer near-instant delivery of popular products, it is not their core business model. Instacart's service areas across the US make it a reliable mechanism for brands to offer two-hour delivery of their products.

Use cases for Instacart

In closing this chapter, here are a handful of ways that brands can find the most effective business case for Instacart.

1. Focus on actively promoting the 'fat head' product assortment, not the 'long tail'. Your top-selling products are more likely to end up as repeat purchases, further solidifying their placement in future searches and purchases. Double down on these.

2. Smaller brands can use Instacart to gain competitive advantage over big brands, as potential replacements. Smaller brands can use their ability to make faster decisions and decide to switch gears with promotional approaches. Also, as discussed further in chapter 5, smaller brands can potentially access the same or better advertising and reporting tools as big advertisers, due to a tiering system that provides increasing levels of data for brands who spend more on advertising.

3. Double down on Instacart a few days before major holidays and events that are relevant to your brand — their fast delivery works well for last-minute customers. Instacart has recognized this opportunity and encourages customers to give Instacart gift cards to friends and family to aid holiday shopping through the platform. Those gift cards are then used in the following weeks.

4. Smaller retailers and retail chains who can't afford to invest in their own last-mile delivery

infrastructure can use Instacart to expand their service offering. We discuss the relationship that retailers have with Instacart in detail in chapter 10.

5. Similarly, brands themselves can leverage Instacart as a third party provider of two-hour delivery. Even brands with scaled direct to consumer infrastructure like e.l.f Cosmetic can use Instacart to direct customers who want immediate delivery of an item.

6. Grocery brands can use Instacart as an alternative to Amazon Fresh in some markets. A footprint of Amazon Fresh distribution centers is currently limited, which means that it is not available to shoppers in many US cities. Instacart has an advantage here, as it partners with hundreds of retailers across the US. Moreover, the Amazon Fresh team has a notorious reputation for negotiating fiercely with brands and requesting significant co-op fees and marketing spend — in some cases requesting more than the brand's total sales on Fresh, says Melissa Burdick from Pacvue. Burdick says that this opportunity with Instacart opens up more competition and more opportunities for brands.

ON OCTOBER 14TH 2020, Instacart published an interesting story about how their search algorithm is optimized for misspellings. A while ago, a simple misspelling on Instacart like "Avacado" would result in no product results, which is creates a poor customer experience.

Fun fact: other common misspellings on Instacart include Siracha, Zuchinni, Jalepeno, Cantelope, Parmesean

While grammar nuts might applaud this no-tolerance policy to typos, it was undoubtedly hurting sales.

. . .

In the past, the team at Instacart corrected these misspellings manually, but as the company grew, they developed a complex machine-learning algorithm to fix the problem.

This is testament to the scale that Instacart has built into its search and advertising algorithm. Attracting and keeping advertising dollars from large and small companies alike requires constant improvement and innovation, and while we see only one type of advertising campaign at the time of writing, our view is that Instacart's advertising capabilities will explode in the next couple of years. This chapter serves as a primer on the infrastructure of Instacart's demand generation levers outside of advertising, how brands are maximizing their ROI, and what's likely to come next.

Key Driver 1: Instacart's search algorithm

Each major marketplace has its own tightly-held search algorithm. Amazon's is called "A9" and while the algorithm factors are a secret and in constant flux, much study on search ranking results confirms that the main factors are: product content (presence of relevant keywords in titles and descriptions), product listing performance metrics (sales velocity, conversion rate), and seller performance metrics (fulfillment method etc).

With Instacart being a newer platform with fewer APIs, we know less about its internal mechanisms for deciding how to organize hundreds for SKUs when a customer searches for generic terms like "crackers" or "nude lipstick". Here's what we know so far:

- Independent third-party advertising solutions that utilize Instacart's API are the most impacted when an algorithm changes. Ad-tech firm Pacvue was one of Instacart's earliest API partners in 2020. Co-Founder and President, Melissa Burdick, says that Instacart's algorithm is constantly changing, and that they see a lot of ongoing testing.
- Instacart's Data Science team works on two main aspects of the Instacart experience: Fulfillment, and Search and Personalization.
- Instacart's search algorithm has another level of complexity than those at Amazon or Walmart: it has to check for product availability across many retail partners inventory levels, not their own data. The algorithm gets updated hourly. "We predict the availability of over 500 million listings every 60 minutes," said the Instacart Engineering team in 2020. Instacart's availability and replacement components make the algorithm very different from those at Amazon and Walmart: Instacart's is more influenced by customer's past behaviours and product availability, and has no equivalent component of star ratings or reviews.
- Instacart's search algorithm is location-based. When a user accesses the site and enters their zip code, only the nearby retail partners are taken into consideration when displaying available products. This makes the point about

brands needing alignment with their retail partners all the more important: you could miss out on key geographies if your local retailers are not engaged with Instacart, or feeding accurate inventory information. There is a ton of room for error here. Retailer inventory systems are known to often be very inaccurate.

- Each Instacart listing has four main parameters. These are the attributes that brands and retailers should ensure are kept up to date: Name; Product ID; Several sub-attributes like departments, aisle numbers, dietary/cuisine tags; Nutritional information.

- In addition to categorical data, Instacart also collects historical data for a given product listing.

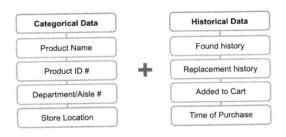

With this data, two models in particular work hand-in-hand to ensure a smooth customer and shopper experience: the Item Availability Model and the Replacement Recommendation Model.

1. The Item Availability Model relies on historical retailer availability data, store location, an item's purchase history,

and shopper inputs to predict the likelihood that a particular item in the catalog is or isn't in stock at any one of nearly available physical stores.

2. If an item receives a low availability score, the Replacement recommendation model takes over. It fires up a flow in the app asking customers to pre-select a replacement as they browse.

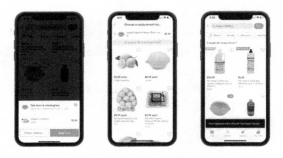

Above: Instacart app's product replacement interface

"Our current model relies on a combination of categorical data like product names and an item's replacement history to draw invisible lines between related item listings and stack rank potential replacements," explains the Instacart Engineering Team in a blog post.

This opens up an opportunity for some brands to compete on the grounds of product availability. Simply having better availability improves the probability of products becoming replacements for similar out-of-stock alternatives. We cover how brands can affect availability later in the book.

. . .

A great deal of purchasing flows from repeated purchases (the "Your Items" navigation section) rather than search, as we discuss in detail in the following section.

Instacart's search algorithm is highly personalized

Jeremy Stanley, ex-VP of Data Science at Instacart, says: "At a physical grocery store, you have to discover new products on your own. But at Instacart, we can curate the experience for you through personalization. We have more density on our user behavior than any ecommerce company I have ever seen. We are just beginning to use that data to provide incredibly valuable personalized experiences for our users on Instacart in search, in product discovery and in suggestions we make to our users."

We think that the heavy reliance on the personalization aspect of Instacart's search algorithm gives smaller brands a fighting chance; they can be among the top search results for Instacart customers that prefer them.

The bottom line is that product availability will make or break your Instacart success. The implications of out-of-stock are even more serious than on Amazon, since Instacart will actively promote alternatives to ensure the customers don't leave empty-handed.

. . .

What Instacart's algorithm is programmed to solve

Haixun Wang, Instacart's VP of Algorithms, wrote a blog post in 2018 detailing the current limitations of the existing "search-click-ship" ecommerce model. Potential solutions, according to Wang, include the following:

- Investing in intent-based searches. For example as of 2018 when Wang wrote his post, "red wine $30" yielded poor results in most ecommerce search engines except for Google, who understands the three separate keywords to signify intent of purchasing a bottle of red wine at a $30 price point.
- Visual search, where a user provides a picture and gets products that look similar to the picture, or the algorithm serves similar results based on what a user has indicated interest in.
- Aggregating outside information sources to address research-based queries. Wang says that for queries such as "insomnia", many ecommerce search engines do not provide relevant results although there is plenty of information on the web that could help a purchasing decision.
- Conversational and voice-assisted commerce.
- Delineating between product-based queries, and need-based queries. What are the product alternatives that could be served?
- Serendipity. Customers visit malls even if they have nothing to buy — they are hoping to be inspired. This 'serendipitous' shopping rarely occurs on ecommerce marketplaces like

Amazon and Walmart. "E-tailers should endeavor to inform, inspire, enlighten and entertain its customers," Wang says.

These give us some insights into what the top algorithm expert at Instacart had on his mind back in 2018. But regardless of the future changes of the algorithm, we like to go back to the core of what a given platform is trying to accomplish. With Instacart, we believe that its algorithms are being developed based on two pillars: impeccable customer experience and the shortest path to purchase, allowing customers to buy with as few clicks as possible. Brands who optimize their Instacart channel strategy with these key points in mind will win.

Key demand driver 2: Repeat purchases

Amazon is known for its "flywheel" of digital disruption: a virtuous cycle that spins ever faster due to its low product prices, high volume of buyers, and increasing numbers of sellers who want to engage with those customers, thus increasing competition and assortment and further lowering prices.

Instacart has its own flywheel effect: repeat purchases. Repeat purchases are the holy grail of ecommerce, since customer acquisition costs are generally a key expense. Retaining an existing customer, increasing purchase frequency, and increasing basket size are the preferred ways of growing revenue for any e-tailer. From this perspective, Instacart is onto a winner:

- 90% of Instacart's customers are repeat customers.
- Express customers (Instacart's membership program) spend an average of $500 a month.
- 20-25% of Instacart shopping activity comes from repurchasing, according to a webinar presentation given to brand and agency advertisers in Q4 2020.

Instacart's unique ability to prompt repurchases lights a fire under brands: you must get into the customers' basket *now*. Brands who are savvy enough to move fast and adopt an Instacart strategy which results in sales now can reap the rewards for years to come in the form of repeated purchases. These are organic sales that you don't have to pay for in the long term.

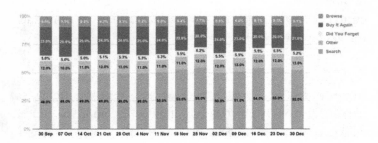

A time series showing the source of purchased products, shared by Instacart with advertisers in a webinar in Q4,

2020. A large percentage of purchases comes from a "buy it again" prompt.

Encouraging browsing

Brands like Clif Bar have seen a lot more browsing-type behavior on Instacart and other retailer sites, compared with Amazon. Instacart, like many other retail platforms, requires a minimum purchase threshold to get free shipping. This type of set-up inspires customers to browse more on the platform, because even if they only need an item or two, they are looking for additional items to purchase to fill out their basket and qualify for free shipping.

This type of behaviour justifies investment in banner advertising, as banners and other display type ad units are a good way to create brand awareness and educate customers about new products.

Key demand driver 3: Optimizing product content

Instacart currently does not have a self-serve content management capability for brands to add and update product content. This is a major shortcoming for a lot of brands, who are seeing great results from optimizing product content on Amazon.

"There's a key reason why product content is a core piece of Amazon's algorithm. It drives discovery, conversion, and customer delight. And it's not just the basics, its content assets that establish the brand. Accuracy, completeness are the minimally viable requirements for driving search, and below the fold experience drives conversion."

— Peter Crosby, VP of Corporate Marketing at Salsify and Executive Director at the Digital Shelf Institute

Currently, Instacart charges retailers a setup fee to load up product content including images and nutrition panels. Our view is that this is a sub-optimal approach. In fact, we have found some cursory product searches on Instacart to return factually incorrect information about certain products (for example a can of Pringles revealed a 2.3oz can incorrectly titled as 2.6oz despite the image being 2.3oz). This is a risk for brands, retailers, and Instacart when products could include misleading product information.

Instacart would greatly benefit from providing brands with the ability to edit product content, as brands are generally best placed to add product keywords and additional images beyond the main thumbnail.

We do expect that brands will be given a self-service option in the near future, and there is an existing work-around that exists today. Some brands are using software like Salsify, which combines its Product Information Management (PIM) system with content syndication capabilities to optimize and share product listing content across all relevant ecommerce platforms. Salsify is the only solution we're familiar with that currently has this capability with Instacart.

Julie Liu from CLIF BAR says that her company has been working with a software solution since Q2 of 2020 to syndicate product content to Instacart. "Otherwise," she says, "It would just be too much of a manual hassle for us to manage retailers, UPC codes, and availability."

The implication of this current situation is that brands either need to invest in a PIM with content syndication capabilities like Salsify, or rely on their retail partners to invest in Instacart product content.

Key demand driver 4: Coupons and delivery promotions

Two of the marketing tools Instacart offers to brands are delivery promotions and coupons. Delivery promotions are discounts on delivery fees that are funded by a manufacturer when a customer orders qualifying items from that manufacturer, and coupons are a manufacturer's coupons that are automatically applied to qualifying products. These promotions can be displayed on the product thumbnail and a "Savings" tab in the store navigation.

This is a tactic that PepsiCo has relied on in the past, says Christina Vail, Director, Client Strategy at Profitero. Pepsi, with its vast house of brands, could create a "buy five items, get free delivery" promotion, and get Tropicana juice,

Quaker cereal, Pepsi soft drink, and Lay's chips all in the customer's basket and "Bought Before" list. These are above-the-line marketing dollars that are being spent to prompt future purchases of these items — an investment that could pay off for years.

Brands that operate in a single category, like CLIF BAR, can also see good results by making a 'portfolio play'. "Our products are all within the same category: bars and snacks," Says Julie Liu. "Whereas when I talk to other manufacturers [who have items across various categories] the delivery promotions aren't as effective, because there's not a direct correlation in the consumer's mind to make a purchase with all those products added together."

High-growth health and wellness brand Simple Mills decided to participate in a 'Spend $15 Get $5' program with Instacart with the goals of increasing revenue, spend per delivery, and items per cart in mid-December 2020. Comparing averages from the prior 13 week period, Simple Mills found:

- A 58% increase in overall sales
- A 20% increase in spend per delivery
- A 23% increase in items in cart

Overall, the company saw more than a 2x return on investment, with increased sales volume creating a positive impact on customer lifetime value.

. . .

Another strategy that brands are using is to combine coupons and delivery promotions with banner advertising to get ahead on Instacart. Ingrid Milman Cordy, Head of Digital and eCommerce at Nuun Hydration, says that the health brand sees a measurable impact with this strategy, and is currently testing the relative effectiveness of running a banner ad before, during or after a coupon campaign. Milman Cordy's current approach is to stage the timing:

> "Let's say you're running the coupon for a week and you have a banner placement for two weeks, I would have [the banner ad] running the week before, and then have it running the week during [the coupon] so you have a baseline and you've set the [customer's] intention there with the banner for a week, and the week after you have [the banner ad] supporting the coupon."

Delivery promotions and coupons are larger investments for most brands, and operate as a managed service by Instacart — not a self-service model as exists on Amazon. This makes it harder for brands to experiment with delivery promotions as a marketing tactic.

The general consensus from brands that we've spoken with is that delivery promotions fall behind Featured Product advertising in terms of ROI.

Key Driver 5: Inventory availability

Since Instacart carries no inventory of its own, it is

dependent on the retailers having stock available for the products that customers are searching for. If a retailer flunks their projections of what's necessary, both the retailer and the manufacturer will lose out on potential sales.

Known out-of-stock items will not show up in search, either paid or organic. Instacart's operations team works with retailers to make sure they have the most up-to-date inventory counts. Instacart's in-store shoppers essentially function as auditors of this information. If an item is unable to be found the shopper will reach out to the customer to find a suitable replacement.

But even within this paradigm, some manufacturers are able to exert more control than others. As Christina Vail, Director of Client Strategy at ecommerce analytics firm Profitero explains:

"There is a cohort of manufacturers that have direct store delivery capabilities, and therefore have a direct way to impact their on shelf availability at a door-by-door, store-by-store level. I think a lot of manufacturers are really trying to understand how they can get better at sensing and responding to supply chain complexities when local stores are now being expected to support online and in-store demand."

Direct store delivery — whereby a manufacturer is responsible for inventory storage and delivery instead of third-party shippers — is not a silver bullet. You still need the retailer to place adequate purchase orders, and setting up such a system is costly and complex. But it can help manufacturers with improving store-level availability, as the retailer is now no longer responsible for moving inventory around its network, and the average inventory turn-around can be much faster.

A better in-stock rate than your competitors will put you ahead both within the search experience, and also when a shopper is in-store filling a cart for the end customer. Many shoppers and customers open a chat to agree on replacement items if anything is out of stock. One customer on Twitter congratulated their shopper for proactively asking if the customer wanted some Lysol wipes, which were miraculously in-stock at a store during the pandemic. And as we discuss elsewhere in this book, conversational commerce is a natural extension for Instacart, with shoppers not just taking orders but giving tips and suggestions for customers.

Pilot features

Instacart appears to pilot new features with select brands on a managed service basis before rolling the features out to more brands and/or as a self-serve option. So it's helpful to keep up to date with the current pilot programs as a means of understanding what is likely coming down the pipe in the future. (Our newsletter at www.bobsledmarketing.com is a great start.)

. . .

One brand we spoke with told us about three programs that are in the pilot stage:

- An email marketing capability, which would go hand in hand with Delivery Promotions
- Search keyword banners with a cost-per-click fee model (performance-based)
- Storefronts on the homepage that drive to product pages, with an impression-based fee model

Intermediary solutions to drive traffic to Instacart

Brands want to support retailers. Brands, in addition to selling products to major retailers (Walmart, Kroger, Target) can improve customer experience for customers visiting the brand website. Beauty brand e.l.f. utilizes a third party solution to add a Buy via Instacart button to their website, which uses the customer's zip code to recommend Instacart supported stores nearby, thus supporting their major retailer partners.

e.l.f. initiated a software solution called MikMak to drive traffic from its digital advertising to whichever marketplace or retailer the customer would prefer to transact on, whether that's Amazon, Ulta, or Instacart. Molly Dufner, VP Ecommerce and Customer Experience at e.l.f. says that the company is also experimenting with the same technology on the product pages on its own website: offering customers the ability to purchase directly from e.l.f., or to "get it today from Instacart". Since e.l.f. Cosmetics products are sold at major retailers like CVS, this creates a way for the company to offer their products immediately to customers when they wouldn't otherwise be able to do so.

"We have all these great customers, we have a loyalty program, and we want to be able to give them new, and innovative ways that they can get our products. So for us, it's not about only selling on our direct to consumer site. It's about how we can use digital and innovation to grow our sales across every point of where we sell our product."

— Molly Dufner, e.l.f Cosmetics

Demand generation on Instacart is in many ways an entirely different beast to other ecommerce marketplaces. The core of the difference is the presence of a stakeholder that is usually absent: the retailer. In its current incarnation, branded manufacturers must rely on Instacart for product content and inventory availability — two significant drivers of purchasing behavior. This is where branded manufacturers really must get on the same page as their retail partners, to understand their ordering logic, their current and planned relationship with Instacart, and how you as the manufacturer might be able to more directly influence inventory availability.

We expect manufacturers to be able to exert more control over the buying experience on Instacart in the future. The key will be to follow developments closely and understand how changes can be leveraged to drive first-time orders and repeat orders.

As it stands, the current state highlights a need for digital shelf solutions like that monitor product content compliance and product availability. A PIM like Salsify can syndicate the content across marketplaces, but brands will also want to track product availability and content compliance through an analytics tool like Profitero.

THE TIMING of the launch of Instacart's Featured Products ad type could not have been better. In March of 2020, Instacart had just started capturing the attention of marketing and ecommerce executives, due to its rapid customer acquisition in the early days of the COVID-19 pandemic. Instacart was an essential service that millions of North Americans could use to reliably purchase grocery items. Within a few weeks of introducing the Featured Products advertising API to a small number of software firms, Instacart became the hot new advertising platform that CPG brands were diverting their now-useless shopper marketing ad budgets toward.

But Instacart's fledgling advertising solution is far more than just hype. All of the brands we spoke with who are running Instacart performance advertising as well as advertising on other ecommerce marketplaces report a great ROAS with their Instacart ads.

.   .   .

While 2020 was a year of experimentation for the early adopters, beyond 2020, it is imperative that brands develop an independent Instacart strategy that will work for them.

In this chapter, we will give a detailed overview of Instacart's main (and currently only) self-service ad unit, Featured Products; compare Instacart's advertising solutions with Amazon, discuss three key limitations of Instacart advertising as it currently stands, and conclude with our view of what's to come.

Featured Products

Targeting potential customers closer to the bottom of the advertising funnel, Featured Products are keyword-targeted advertising campaigns that allow advertisers to bid on relevant keywords and promote products related to those search terms.

For example, a supplements manufacturer could bid on a variety of search terms like "melatonin", "sleeping pills", or "insomnia".

Featured Products advertising placements on Instacart are almost indistinguishable from organic results — the only difference is the "Featured" label in the top left corner. The first three results for any search are Featured Products (similar to a Google search) which is priceless ecommerce real estate. According to information shared by Instacart with brand advertisers, 70% of purchase conversions take place in the first row of search results.

Use Cases: Why would brands bid on keywords on Instacart?

Keyword level bidding allows brands to:

- Appear in favorable search placements by bidding on keywords relevant to the products they are promoting.
- Attract new mid-funnel and lower-funnel potential customers who are looking to fill a need rather than for a specific product.
- Capture market share by having their ads appear when a potential customer searches for a competitive product.

How Instacart's Featured Product auction works

Featured Products are an auction-based advertising unit, meaning that the highest bidder will win the placement. Instacart determines a winning bid with the following formula, starting with a predicted click through rate (CTR) which is not shown to the advertiser.

Predicted CTR (click through rate) * CPC bid amount = overall expected value. Highest expected value will receive the better placement.

The auction is a second price auction, similar to Amazon's format. A second price auction means the winning bidder pays only one cent more than the second highest bidder. For example: if the winning bidder's bid for a given keyword is $1, and the second highest bid is $0.75, the winner will pay $0.76 for that click.

The only targeting option: Keyword Targeting

Featured Products currently only has one way to target customers: keyword targeting. Keywords are the search terms (singular words or phrases) that customers type into Instacart's search bar when looking for a particular product.

The bid is the highest amount of money an advertiser is willing to pay for a given click. Advertisers set bids on an ad group (a group of relevant keywords) or a single keyword level.

. . .

Keyword-level bids are used in auctions for search placements tied to a specific keyword or string of keywords. For example, "melatonin" might be a single keyword-level bid, with its own market-determined price or cost-per-click (CPC).

For all other non-search placements, Instacart uses the default "ad group" CPC. Auctions are still won based on a combination of CPC bid and relevancy.

Scenario	Bid taken into consideration by Instacart
Customer searches for a keyword (e.g. "melatonin") and clicks on a product promoted by a particular advertiser.	Bid set on a single keyword level
Customer clicks on a product outside of a keyword search scenario (e.g. scrolling through popular items, browsing within departments, Instacart editorial content, item details, in the personalized "Your Items" section, etc.)	Bid set on an ad group level

Above: bidding scenarios

Instacart also will only serve Featured Products to users who are in a location where that SKU is in stock at a local retailer. This geo-targeting is entirely dependent on the customer's zip code; advertisers have no control over it. This has the benefit of establishing a guardrail against wasted ad spend, and also prevents advertisers from circumventing Instacart's limits on advertising only with specific retailers (whereby a certain geography might only include a single retailer for a given product category).

. . .

Other keyword rules:

- A maximum of 1,000 keywords can be supported in an Ad Group
- Any word or phrase is eligible (including competitor searches)
- Ads with keyword-level bids will be subject to the same platform bid minimums as ads with default ad group bids

The verdict from brands

While Featured Products is in its infancy (just 12 months old as of time of writing), there's good reasons why Instacart became one of the hottest advertising channels for CPG brands in 2020.

Extensive reach

Instacart's delivery capabilities reaches 85% of US households, and customer order volume shot up up by 500% within the space of a year[1] — that's a lot of customers that brands can reach.

Instacart also aggregates over 500 retailers (and seven out of ten of the top US retailers) onto a single platform, allowing brands to allocate ad spend to their entire retailer network with a single investment.

NRF 2020 Rank	Company	Instacart relationship
1	Walmart	Yes (pilot in select markets)
2	Amazon.com	No
3	The Kroger Co.	Yes
4	Costco	Yes
5	Walgreens Boots Alliance	Yes
6	The Home Depot	No
7	CVS Health Corporation	Yes
8	Target	Yes
9	Lowe's Companies	No
10	Albertsons Companies	Yes

Above: Analysis of Instacart availability by NRF 2020 Rank [2]

Higher advertising-attributed sales

Many brands we spoke with are seeing a higher percentage of sales come through from advertising on Instacart compared to what they see on Amazon.

Todd Hassenfelt, Senior Director of Ecommerce at Simple Mills, says that about half of his company's sales are attributed to search, compared with Amazon, where it's about 20% to 25% on average.

. . .

Why is this a good thing? On one hand, it is hard to swallow that you're spending money to acquire half of your sales. But what this offers advertisers today is effectiveness of reach. And even better, what it offers tomorrow is those same products being in the "Your Items" section of a customer's app over a long time period. Add to the fact that many advertisers are seeing exceptional ROAS, many advertisers see higher effectiveness of reach with Instacart right now.

Great ROI

All brands that we have spoken with who are actively advertising on Instacart say that Featured Products are very profitable and generate strong return on advertising investment, especially compared to Amazon. Jim Morgan from Vita Coco points out that it is not uncommon to hear of $10+ in returns for every dollar spent, with many companies in their category and adjacent categories seeing a 1:10 ROAS on Instacart. We expect that this is mainly driven by the lack of competition compared to more established online grocery platforms.

While the CPCs are increasing — especially on competitive search terms — they are still far below what we see on more developed and competitive platforms like Amazon. In many cases, CPC is 50% lower on Instacart than for the same keyword on Amazon.[3]

Still, relying on ROI alone is a very narrow view of analyzing the advertising impact. The question asked of every advertising agency is whether they can improve the client's ROAS. It's certainly possible by focusing bids on hyper-specific branded search terms that have already proven to convert. But smart brands already know this, and are more interested in the incremental growth of total sales driven by advertising rather than doubling down on expensive and narrow options.

> "When we look at efficiency in terms of incrementality compared to baseline trends, Instacart's Featured Product offering has proven to be successful in converting new households."

— Julie Liu, Clif Bar & Company

Smart brands establish a baseline of ad-generated sales, and certainly do what they can to make that spend more efficient over time. But they also seek out new platforms, ad types, targeting and other strategies to drive incremental sales over their baseline. Instacart, while offering superior ROAS, also generally offers incremental sales growth to brands, making it attractive on both fronts.

Compare and Contrast: Instacart advertising versus Amazon and Walmart

In the table below we summarize the key technical differences between Instacart, Amazon, and Walmart's advertising platforms.

	Instacart	Amazon	Walmart
Auction Type	Second price auction	Second price auction	First price auction
Ad types available	Featured Products	Sponsored Products, Sponsored Brands, Sponsored Display	Sponsored Product
Charging method	Cost per click	Cost per click / Cost per impression	Cost Per Click
Targeting Options	Keyword Targeting	Keyword Targeting, Product (ASIN) Targeting, Category Targeting, Audience Targeting	Keyword Targeting
Auto Targeting	Yes	Yes	Yes
Ad groups available	Yes	Yes	Yes

In building its advertising machine, Instacart has hired many executives who have worked on other major advertising platforms. Seth Dallaire, the Chief Revenue Officer of Instacart, previously held the post of Vice President of Global Advertising Sales at Amazon. Instacart's Chief Technology Officer, Mark Schaaf, was a senior engineering director in the early days of Google's mobile display ads. This legacy assumes that a lot of lessons learned from the two major advertising platform incumbents will be brought across to Instacart, both in terms of developing a leading advertising solution, and in selling it effectively to brands and agencies.

But in terms of advertising dollar spend, Instacart has a lot of ground to make up. All brands that we have spoken with are still investing significantly more on Amazon than Instacart. This is due to three key factors: inability to target retailer and geography, internal channel ownership, and inability to target customers based on behavioral activity.

. . .

In the next section we'll expand on these limitations.

Limitation 1: Inability to target retailer and geography

Instacart's main differentiator at the moment is that the served ads depend on a logged-in user's zip code. This helps both customers and brands since it only serves ads for products in stock, located in supported retailers close to the user's zip code. This guardrail limits wasted ad spend for the brand for products that aren't in stock.

But there is a big opportunity that brands are frustrated not to be able to execute on: being able to run ads against a specific retailer. For example, a CPG brand might be particularly interested in targeting Wegmans customers — this might be because the brand knows that Wegmans customers are more likely to convert, or it could be that the brand wants to demonstrate advertising commitment to Wegmans as a key account. At least for now, this capability does not exist.

Dean McElwee, Integrated Commercial Lead of E-Commerce for Europe at the Kellogg Company, says that this a serious limitation because CPGs decide investment strategy on a "where to play" basis. An investment strategy is driven by business-critical factors such as strategic intent, profitability of the retail account, and the fit of the retailer's customers. The fact that Instacart cannot or will not publish retailer-level data throws a huge spanner in the works of these strategic factors.

. . .

Instacart also does not provide an ability to target by geography. Geo-targeting, otherwise known as local PPC, refers to the practice of delivering different content or advertisements to consumers based on their geographic locations.

It's interesting that this feature does not yet exist, given that ad serving is already localized. A logged-in user will only see ads for products that are in-stock at a store in a nearby zip code. So while the ability to geo-target exists, Instacart has not turned on this feature for advertisers, and it is not mentioned on Instacart's feature roadmap for the first half of 2021. Of its competitors, Amazon DSP (demand side platform — Amazon's display advertising solution) offers a geo-targeting solution to reach audiences based on certain zip codes.

Speculatively, both of these points could be related to the relationship between Instacart and retailers. Instacart and retailers are competing for manufacturer ad dollars. If Instacart allows brands to target certain retailers or geographies (whereby a certain geography might only include a single retailer for a given product category), then Instacart is directly stemming the flow of advertising dollars away from retailers. With retailers still critical to Instacart's success, they can't afford to be off-side.

Limitation 2: Confusion about Instacart ownership bleeds into Instacart advertising

In many companies, multiple internal teams are responsible for handling various components of the Instacart relationship. There is a danger of a short-sightedness towards measuring the impact and ROI of Instacart advertising.

John Denny, VP eCommerce & Digital Marketing at CAVU Venture Partners says that objectives and skill sets vary dramatically between internal teams like shopper marketing and ecommerce, and their broader sales and marketing divisions.

Downstream branding impacts can be even more critical than the immediate return on ad spend, but the paradigm for most consumer brands is a singular focus on ROAS for the ecommerce team. As such, a problem can exist with both under-investing and over-spending on Instacart.

Limitation 3: Inability to target based on customer purchase habits and previous interaction with the brand

As advertising platforms like Amazon mature, they are able to target more sophisticated behavioral associations like which users are "in-aisle" of a certain department, at the research stage of their buying journey, and customers who frequently purchase from another brand.

Since Instacart could eventually amass a quantity of actual purchasing history to rival Amazon, this presents a huge opportunity for behavioral, demographic, and interest-based targeting.

> "I would love to invest in marketing tactics that have targeted capabilities based on purchase and browsing behavior. Instead of running general coupons across the platform, I'd prefer to offer a targeted digital coupon to buyers of a certain competitor or across our category."

— Julie Liu, Clif Bar & Company

Another limitation that frustrates brands is the lack of a rating and review capability. This was noted as a significant 'miss' in the view of some brands given how important ratings and reviews are in the consumer journey. As it stands, an Instacart shopper might navigate out of the app to an alternative channel like Amazon to check reviews of a new product before purchasing.

Todd Hassenfelt from Simple Mills says that since consumers discover new brands and products when shopping online, product reviews could greatly help Instacart to gain and retain more customers. A review sharing or syndication program with retailer partners could solve this issue quickly.

What's coming next

Instacart has aggressive growth goals for its advertising business. A job advertisement for a Director of Data

Science on Instacart's website says, "In this position, you will work closely with senior product and engineering leadership to **grow and drive Instacart's ads revenue into a multi-billion dollar business**," and also that the role would help Instacart to "**5x our ads revenue over the next 2-3 years**"[4] (Emphasis added.)

Instacart clearly has the ambition to grow into a significant advertising platform. And while it has proven immense ROI in performance advertising, more leverage exists outside of just an algorithmic search advertising vehicle. There are a few ways we see this shift unfolding.

- Instacart could make a play towards introducing more middle- and top-of-funnel self-serve advertising products, given the nature of advertisers on its platform (mid to large brands). Advertising on Instacart is retailer-agnostic, and it would provide brands with a neat solution to shift a portion of their branding budget towards Instacart.
- Instacart could build very creative, 'editorial' type ad units. In an interview, Vikaram Gupta, Instacart's Vice President of Ads Engineering, says that in the longer term, he is "dreaming about how to bring more inspirational content into the ads."[5] We could see CPG brands publishing recipes in collaboration with a celebrity chef, or a baby care brand sharing top tips for new moms.

- More near-term, we believe that self-serve banners will be Instacart's first top-of-funnel solution released on the platform. During 2020, brands had the option to create banner campaigns working with Instacart's support team. That's often the sign of a feature that will be rolled out on a self-serve capacity.

"Banners are a good way for us to drive awareness and gain exposure within the category for people who are browsing in addition to using the search function. We definitely see banner investments as more of an awareness play versus direct sales driving."

— Julie Liu, Clif Bar & Company

Taking action

We've passed rather quickly through a few stages in this chapter: an introduction to existing capabilities, an exploration of limitations, and some speculation on where Instacart could take its solution next. It should be clear that we believe Instacart to be a viable performance-oriented advertising platform that's suitable for many consumer brands to start working with right now.

As Melissa Burdick, Co-Founder and President of ad-tech solution Pacvue, says: "[Instacart] is low competition, with a lot of demand and traffic coming. And that equals a high return on ad spend which is another reason to get somewhere first."

So what's the best way for brands to get started now? Stefan, whose entire career has been dedicated to performance marketing, shares his recommended approach below.

1. Before you get started with Featured Products: get feedback from the sales team within your company about current and expected inventory availability. Also consider revisiting the forecasting models — you have to now account for the impact of trade spend in store and marketing spend on Instacart to model inventory needs out.

2. Invest in Featured Products as early as possible. There is undoubtedly a first-mover advantage at the moment. Hot tip: Instacart can provide brand-specific customer lifetime value data to validate the importance of getting in early on Featured Products to help secure investments internally.

3. Get internal agreement on overall advertising priorities: are you wanting to aggressively grow market share, or maintain a specific level of profitability? Each priority will dictate a different bidding and campaign strategy.

4. Rely on lessons learned from other ecommerce platforms, Amazon and Walmart in particular. Start with converting search terms on Amazon, utilize competing SKUs as guides towards

discovering your products value adds over competitor products.

5. Select an ad-tech partner that will meet your current needs around automating bidding, building campaigns, generating reports etc. Make sure your chosen ad-tech partner is committed to investing in Instacart capabilities.

6. Consider the keywords that you'll be bidding on through the full customer purchase journey: conquesting and defending your brand search terms, acquiring market share from competitors, driving awareness of your product, driving awareness of the solution. Consider setting up an analytics solution to monitor your own availability, as well as out-of-stock issues with competitors. Conquesting out-of-stock competitors can be a successful tactic.

7. Combine Featured Products and coupons to improve click through rates. This means you're paying for advertising as well as funding a discount on the coupon, so you'll need to do the math to figure out your break-even point. But we find that this strategy dramatically improves click through rate and conversion rates, and Amazon recognized this strategy and made it a native feature in Q4 of 2020.

8. Be sure to select as many ad slots as Instacart offers (currently the number is three) so that competitors cannot sneak in.

9. Think about your own grocery list — do you choose by brand or by product type? Do you use a branded or unbranded search term for this

product type? Keep that in mind when advertising.

10. Consider working with an agency like Bobsled Marketing to save time, stay up-to-date on all new advertising releases, and work on customizable solutions directly with Instacart.

PART 4

PART IV: WHERE DOES INSTACART FIT IN MY COMPANY?

THE FOLLOWING phrase is frequently spotted throughout Instacart's public terms and conditions of service: "Instacart is not a retailer or seller."

And the brand that has products available to purchase on Instacart is also not a seller. Contrast this to Amazon or Walmart — where those entities could be the seller (in the case of a 1P relationship) or the brand could be the seller (in the case of the a 3P relationship). With Instacart, brands are heavily reliant on their retail partners to make their assortment available, set prices, invest in product content, and more fundamentally, to choose whether to even engage with Instacart.

Contrary to an assumption that Instacart is just another ecommerce platform that can be delegated to the ecommerce or digital department, Instacart is just as much a game of stakeholder engagement with retail partners as it is about improving return on ad spend.

Our conversations with brands on this topic surfaced significant concerns from brands about where Instacart appears in their company records: both in the P&L and in where accountability for performance lies within the organization. In this chapter we'll explore these concerns and how some brands are handling the issues right now.

The P&L challenge with Instacart

The root of the issue is that Instacart sales show up within a manufacturer's brick and mortar retailer accounts, but media spend typically sits with ecommerce or digital teams.

Manufacturers also don't receive sales reporting by retailer, even when they are running performance advertising campaigns. Unless a retailer discloses to the brand what proportion of sales are generated in-store versus on Instacart, a brand will have no way to benchmark performance. As such, the sales generated by Instacart have nowhere logical to sit except at the line item of revenues from retailer accounts.

However, the advertising and promotion elements of Instacart are generally assigned to the ecommerce or digital team. This is a digital shopping channel, after all, and those teams are best trained in performance media and have the context of how other similar digital channels work.

Assigning accountability this way is logical, but problems quickly occur when two departments are accountable for the same goal: growing sales on Instacart. This is particularly pertinent when one of those departments (sales) receives no data on how the goal is progressing, and may sometimes even find themselves working with retailers who actively want to reduce their reliance on Instacart.

Typical organizational structures

We asked the brands that we spoke with about who handles Instacart on their teams, and how this resourcing differs to other their online channels. Mostly we found that there is no single owner for Instacart. This is for a few reasons.

Firstly, Instacart launched its self-serve ad platform in May of 2020 with API partners launching their solutions a couple months later, far after annual budgets for most brands had already been set. So many brands could not allocate budget to Instacart and thus not assign it to anyone.

Secondly, an effective Instacart owner requires insight both on the technical advertising side, as well as on the retailer relationship side. Thus, we see the Instacart function landing in the Sales department, the Marketing department, and there being a great deal of cross-over in between.

. . .

There are various ways that brands have chosen to arrange themselves, each with their pros and cons as we discuss in the following section.

Model 1: Ecommerce or Marketing owns the full relationship

In the case of Simple Mills, the ecommerce team owns the relationship with Instacart. In turn, the ecommerce team is a subset of the marketing team.

The benefit here is that the ecommerce team is knowledgeable about optimizing performance marketing, and search advertising in particular. They can transfer knowledge and data from other ecommerce platforms they advertise on.

> "From a control or authority perspective, it probably should be with the commerce team, or whoever is managing Amazon. This way you have the knowledge base of the kind of online searches and how customers search."

— Todd Hassenfelt, Senior Ecommerce Director, Simple Mills

Clif Bar & Company also made the decision to align Instacart with their marketing team since they cannot categorize Instacart as a customer.

"We have been treating Instacart more as a marketing platform rather than a retailer. That's primarily driven by the fact that they don't break out retailer sales, making it difficult for us to attribute sales to a certain account."

— Julie Liu, Shopper Marketing Manager at Clif Bar & Company.

Oshiya Savur, Head of US Marketing and Education at Revlon's Luxury division, also aligns with this logic:

"Instacart is not going to buy product from Revlon, but is instead going to enable revenue through the retailers at which their inventory is already present. Instead, Instacart should be viewed as a media platform similar to how a brand allocates budget to Facebook or Google."

Here are some potential disadvantages of aligning Instacart with the ecommerce or marketing team:

- If the ecommerce team is primarily driven by immediate ROI, it could mean that longer-term branding opportunities are neglected.
- The ecommerce team may not have the same depth of relationship with retailer partners as the sales team, meaning less negotiating power

on important issues like assortment coverage, product content, and pricing.

- There's a disjointed feedback loop: ecommerce runs the campaigns but may not receive news of total sales outcomes from the retail customer.

Model 2: Sales team owns Instacart

Since the sales team owns the relationship with retailers, they have a logical role in managing the Instacart channel. The sales team is aware of the supply chain side of the business: product availability, cost structure for retailers, turn times, etc. They also have deeper relationships with retailers and can lean on this asset to drive sales outcomes that are beneficial both to the retailer and brand (when a product is out of stock on Instacart, it almost certainly means that a product is out of stock in stores). The sales team also has full visibility of other trade promotions in place with retailers, potentially improving marketing spend efficiency as could avoid 'double dipping' on promotional activities.

Aligning Instacart with the sales department creates a closed feedback loop: a single team is running the promotional activities and then getting confirmation from retailer customers about results.

Nuun Hydration is one brand that operates with this setup. The sales team has the accountability of setting and communicating their goals, budgets, and promotional calendars. The marketing and digital media team is then responsible for amplifying those interests and priorities.

> "The sales team not only feel like they have a sense of true ownership over driving traffic to the retailers, but they also want a part of this digital revolution, and I think Instacart does give them that opportunity."

— Ingrid Milman Cordy, Head of Digital and eCommerce at Nuun Hydration.

Here are some potential disadvantages of this setup:

- While the marketing team might prioritize new product introductions where the ROI is poor, the sales team might do the opposite — focusing only on high-ROI assortment and neglecting new products.
- When the sales team is not experienced with digital marketing, it can result in sub-optimal performance of Featured Products, banner ads and other awareness campaigns, and other promotional tools.
- In keeping with what the sales team already knows how to do, the marketing budget might instead be focused on trade-like activities like sponsored delivery promotions, rather than PPC ads or brand campaigns.
- Typically large CPGs would have Grocery, Drug and Mass representatives. Since sales from Instacart are not reported by retailer, it is

not clear which sales team would lead. Since Instacart also has relations with all of these types of retailers, there is confusion about how to decide which team should manage the platform.

- If a retailer is trying to reduce their reliance on Instacart, it might be a contentious decision for the sales team to continue investing in the platform. In this case, it might make the most 'relationship sense' for the ecommerce team to handle the channel so that the decision is viewed as outside of the sales team's hands.

A subset of this scenario is the Shopper Marketing team owning Instacart. But some Shopper Marketing teams are more equipped than others to handle the complexities of the platform. While many brands are led by marketers who have a robust understanding of many digital channels, it's not always the case. Where that skillset has not been developed, it's critical that the responsibility for Instacart is not foisted upon a team without context or expertise in this area. John Denny, VP eCommerce & Digital Marketing at CAVU Venture Partners oversees the ecommerce efforts of portfolio brands like Beyond Meat, Vital Proteins, Bai, and One Bar.

"The challenge I'm seeing right now is shopper marketing teams who are using instacart self serve-tools who know nothing about search and bidding environments who are trying to deal with [Instacart's advertising platform]. And of course, their departments are motivated by immediate return on ad spend. That's the same issue I've seen with ecommerce teams who say 'I can't bid to invest to acquire this customer, because I'm being measured on return on ad spend.'"

Model 3: A hybrid model

Another solution for some brands might lie in a hybrid setup where the ecommerce team owns the performance marketing KPIs, the sales team owns product-related KPIs, and the marketing team owns the branding aspect of advertising with Instacart. If each of these departments don't report up to the same executive, the CMO, CRO and other executive leaders will need to align on accountabilities. It won't necessarily be neat, but it has the benefit of real subject matter experts working on each element for this important and growing channel. Another option is for a matrix-like design, where a core team might be responsible for executing the strategy of a channel, but work closely with internal partners like Sales and Marketing to establish and review KPIs.

Vita Coco currently has a matrix setup, where both marketing and sales provide support on Instacart tasks. Jim Morgan explains:

"[Instacart] sits within the ecommerce team, in the omnichannel subdivision. The omnichannel subdivision then works hand-in-hand with both marketing and sales to support Instacart initiatives."

Similarly, a model that Oshiya Savur at Revlon is considering is a 'core team':

"Media for digital media expertise, ecommerce marketing for content, grocery sales team to identify profitable SKUs and finance to ensure that the KPIs and action standards are clear. Since the channel is growing as fast as it is, it makes sense to stay focused on incremental sales even if that means not optimizing for ROAS."

Todd Hassenfelt from Simple Mills argues for leaders with cross-functional expertise.

"If brands have or can find ecommerce leaders that have both Marketing and Sales department experience, or significant brick and mortar and ecommerce experience, they can bring fair perspective to how to optimize all angles of investment."

Hassenfelt says that these leaders need to act both as coach (for short term wins) and General Manager (for long term vision) to win effectively. But all companies — regardless of having that kind of talent or not — need to ensure Marketing and Sales teams truly work together and understand search campaign expectations and outcomes, so as not to miss revenue and awareness generating activities.

Best practices and things to consider

We wish that there was a straightforward recommendation we could give you about how to set up and account for Instacart within your organization. But the answer is a wholly unsatisfactory "it depends". Many companies (especially larger ones) already have a firm organizational chart of accountabilities, and efforts would be better spent elsewhere than trying to redesign it.

However, there are some clear best practices that we have gleaned from the brands we have spoken and worked with.

- As Julie Liu from CLIF BAR says, "digital is a skill, not a single person's job". The digital or ecommerce team needs to take the time to educate the sales team on ecommerce fundamentals like product availability, content, ratings, reviews, and search.
- To get the rest of their organization on board, ecommerce leaders need to translate ecommerce trends and KPIs into more familiar brick and mortar language.
- Regardless of who "owns" Instacart, ecommerce leaders should guide sales teams on how to

present online opportunities to buyers from
their retail accounts.

- There's rarely an online exclusive shopper or an
in-store exclusive shopper — most shoppers will
move between tools and platforms based on
convenience.
- Having an omnichannel approach allows
activation strategies that have both the physical
and digital element to customers.
- "Ecommerce 'amplifies' and challenges the ways
of working and hence is often seen as an
accelerator of digital transformation," says Dean
McElwee of Kellogg. While it can be painful
and difficult to challenge your company's
existing paradigms, view it as a mechanism to
future-proof your brand.
- Understand that ecommerce is both a marketing
and sales activity — it can't be neatly squared
away into a single division. Partnership across
departments is critical, no matter the
organizational setup.

Consider the following thought experiments:

1. Treat Instacart as a marketing platform like
   Facebook. Instacart is never going to be your
   customer. How would this shift in definition
   change your approach to performance and
   brand marketing initiatives?
2. Think of Instacart as an extension of your brick
   and mortar retail customers. Assortment,

pricing, availability is all controlled by the retailers. How does that change your approach?

3. Does your sales team see digital channels accelerating? They might be just as interested in adapting for the future as the ecommerce team, and welcome opportunities to up-skill in this area.

4. How could success on Instacart positively impact brick & mortar shelf space? This could manifest itself through gaining more space or maintaining existing space during a SKU rationalization.

"ARE you investing in Instacart at the moment? How long have you been working with Instacart?" These were among the first questions we asked experts who were kind enough to share their thoughts with us when this book was in its early planning stage.

Perhaps the best illustration of brands turning to Instacart can be found in the experience of Todd Hassenfelt, the Senior Director of eCommerce of the high-growth health and wellness brand Simple Mills.

Todd told Stefan that Simple Mills was running Featured Product ads when he joined the company in early 2020. "It wasn't because of COVID that we partnered with them. In fact, we have been there since 2018; but it wasn't necessarily a priority."

.   .   .

The first signals of Instacart's rapid upswing came during mid-April of 2020, and Simple Mills' leadership team began hearing how many people relied on Instacart. The company decided that it was time to earnestly start testing and learning on this channel, and started increasing their advertising budget.

"We were seeing that as we were spending more, there was a sales lift," Todd said. "And it was incremental — the spend increases were nominal and that was enough to keep it going."

Most of the brands that we spoke to shared that a significant challenge they face with Instacart relates to understanding the incrementality of the platform. As we have discussed extensively in earlier chapters, Instacart's four-sided marketplace makes it difficult for brands to fully tie back sales results to marketing efforts. But some brands are able to make a strong business case for significantly increased ad spend on Instacart — like high growth health and wellness brand Simple Mills, as we'll cover later.

In this chapter we'll outline the current capabilities that exist within Instacart advertising and analytics, what possibilities exist beyond these native programs, and how other brands are measuring success.

Performance advertising metrics

The impact of Instacart's self-serve Featured Products

can be analyzed through their 'Campaign Manager' dashboard and the data export that can be generated on an aggregated or daily basis.

Above: Instacart's advertising dashboard

Instacart's advertising dashboard provides advertisers with KPIs around spend, attributed sales, attributed quantities, ROAS, impressions, clicks, click through rates, and average cost per click. These are pretty standard advertising metrics; the dashboard does not stand out or offer any unique KPIs unique to Instacart at the moment.

As we discussed earlier in Chapter 7, most brands are seeing a higher ROAS on Instacart than on other marketplaces and advertising platforms, so this lack of detail has been less of a concern from brands to date.

Instacart Customer Intelligence Platform

In addition to performance advertising metrics within the Campaign Manager, Instacart provides brands with Instacart Customer Intelligence Platform (ICIP) reports, which provides brands with data that corresponds with their marketing spend.

ICIP data points include:

- Operations metrics: assortment, distribution, out of stock rates (national, region, city, channel, retailer)
- Sales: sales, share of sales, performance decomposition
- Shopping cart and deliver: new buyer dynamics, basket composition, household penetration, cross shop by brand, basket affinities, path-to-cart
- Customer dynamics: category and brand conversion, trial and repeat, customer lifetime value, new product source of volume

Across the board, brands are interested in gathering more data than Instacart currently provides. The top request by far is for Instacart to split out sales by retailer, but our view is that this is unlikely to happen given Instacart's relationship with retailers.

However, Instacart has mentioned to advertisers that providing more detail and insights for brands is a top priority for the company. Indeed, it would make for a compelling competitive advantage. A well-developed ecosystem exists for brick and mortar retail, with longtime providers like IRI and Nielsen. But many brands find the current ecosystem of solutions for measuring ecommerce market share specifically to be lacking.

Reporting tiers: increased investment means more data

Instacart creates an incentive for brands to spend more on advertising and promotions using a tiering system: the more you spend, the more data you receive. To even out the playing field and afford even small brands the ability to access richer data, Instacart analyzes the marketing investment as a percentage of total sales. Investing 10% or more in Instacart marketing activities unlocks Instacart's full suite of reporting insights available to advertisers large and small. Instacart analyzes spend as a percentage of sales quarterly, and if the required spend to unlock a certain tier is met, the improved reporting is made available the next quarter.

"Spend" can include both self-serve performance advertising and other promotional vehicles like coupons, delivery promotions, and hero banners.

	Tier 3 (5-7.5%)	Tier 2 (7.5-10%)	Tier 1 (>10%)
Frequency	Static Reporting Delivered Monthly (12 periods/year)	Monthly delivery includes breakout by week	Weekly delivery API available
Operations	Assortment, Distribution, Out of Stock at National, Region, Channel	Breakout by geography (by DMA,city)	OOS API available Retailer OOS Available (with approval)
Sales/Share	Sales, Share, Performance Decomposition	Monthly delivery includes breakout by week	Weekly delivery API available
Shopping Cart/ Delivery	New Buyer dynamics Basket + Household Penetration	Basket composition Cross Shop by Brand	Basket Affinities Custom Path to Chart
Customer Dynamics	Category & Brand Conversion Trial and Repeat	LTV Advertising New Product Source of Volume	Custom LTV Analytics

Above: Instacart's Reporting Tiers[1]

In addition to the published tiers, brands that invest seriously with Instacart might also be able to access a 'Joint Business Planning Pilot' for even more first-party data insights.

Simple Mills were reviewing the main KPIs provided by Instacart but were unclear on the incremental sales growth effect of their investment — something that was not provided as a report through with their existing level of spend. Once they unlocked a higher level of reporting, Simple Mills saw enough of a business case to increase their investment by a multi-fold factor. Todd Hassenfelt explains:

"We have increased our investments significantly. This is including COVID stock-up, [but] we're seeing our highest clicks, our highest impressions, and our share of aisle in literally all of our categories at the highest point since we made that increased investment."

Identifying meaningful KPIs

For new platforms like Instacart, the drivers of success might initially be less clear, so it's important to synthesize both your company's overall goals with what data is readily available from the platform or third party providers.

One company that lives and dies by its KPIs is Califia Farms. The plant-based consumables brand established a 'Customer Value Index' — guiding principles that help the brand prioritize activities and make decisions.

Halee Patel, Vice President of Ecommerce at Califia Farms, explained the six values in a webinar:[2]

1. Assortment and Availability: are we available everywhere we are supposed to be (by category, retailer and DTC channels)
2. Ratings: pulse on our customers' sentiment
3. Pricing: issues that can impact profitability
4. Placement: where do we show up and how do we rank
5. Content: are we appropriately educating and speaking to our consumers
6. Sales and Share: keeping a pulse on how we perform vs the category

Califia Farms tracks these business fundamentals daily and weekly through their Profitero dashboard and custom reports. Patel says that the Customer Value Index helped the company to spot some leading indicators of shifting demand, specifically during COVID lockdowns in 2020 when there was a spike in shopper interest for shelf-stable milk products.

Patel says that while the first three values are not yet natively trackable on Instacart, placement, content and sales and share are the best indicators for success.

Another key metric is product content compliance — the percentage of time your product pages are displaying correct images and content. Given the investment of advertising to increase brand awareness, incorrect content can be a big risk, especially for brands that have to be transparent about allergens in food.

Third party scraping tools

One development that we see growing in the future is an ecosystem of independent, third party scraping tools that could provide Instacart advertisers with useful data without requiring large advertising investment.

Many such tools exist for more established marketplaces like Amazon, where third party software tools like Jungle

Scout and Helium10 use a combination of scraping and direct APIs to provide brands and advertisers with data points beyond what Amazon offers, or in a more user-friendly format.

Ecommerce analytics firm Profitero has a digital shelf monitoring solution for Instacart, tracking search of search (paid versus organic), product content compliance, and product availability.

Using Amazon's software and scraper tools ecosystem as a base case, we expect more third party tracking tools to emerge in the future.

Halo and compounding effects

As Kiri wrote about in a post for Forbes titled *The Surprising Impact Of Retail Advertising Investment For Brands,*[3] there is new evidence of a halo effect generated by retail media across all sales channels, online and offline. According to a report by the Digital Shelf Institute in December 2020, $1 invested in marketplace advertising spend returns $7-$10 in brick and mortar retail channels.

While Instacart was not specifically included in the research, it exhibits the same characteristics as more established retail media platforms like Amazon, Walmart and Target.

. . .

Besides the halo effect of sales in the brick and mortar sales channel, we have also heard from many brands who have witnessed high instances of repurchasing in their ICIP reports. A common behavior of Instacart shoppers is to shop from their "Your Items" list of past purchases. So brands that sell replenishable items often see a compounding effect of their marketing efforts over time as customers repeat their past orders.

The CLV (customer lifetime value) data that Instacart provides for your brand, as well as the past purchase data, are also helpful tools to prove this halo effect when executing Featured Products effectively.

What's next for Instacart analytics

While Instacart offers some innovative reporting capabilities and seems to have a strong desire to offer a differentiated analytics platform to brands in the future, a gap exists right now.

"I think the reporting that we've gotten so far is good, but not as robust as we would need for it to be really meaningful. So I think there's definitely room on the reporting side to get better."— Ingrid Milman Cordy, Nuun Hydration

Instacart's reporting has a lot of potential to grow. The current reporting suite fails to capture the incrementality in sales that we see driven by Instacart's performance advertising.

A significant gap that most brands proactively raise is observing retailer-level sales data. Unfortunately we have low confidence in this situation changing due to Instacart's relationships with retailers, which allows retailers to keep this information confidential. It's not in a retailer's interest to give brands data that might create an incentive to stop other forms of shopper marketing or vendor dollar investment in their stores. While Instacart currently provides limited Out Of Stock (OOS) data, providing specifics on where and when OOS occurred could help brands and retail buyers find mutual solutions to ensure products are available to consumers.

Still, accounting for the huge amount of data Instacart collects, we expect they will greatly improve their analytics suite in the near future. Performance against category, customer buying trends to consider, preferred item replacements when a product is out of stock are likely to be among the additions.

"In online grocery, delivery costs are the biggest hurdle to profitability. It's a hurdle that can be overcome only with major investments in advanced analytics, warehouse relocation, and automation. If a grocer isn't willing to go big in ecommerce, it might as well get out".[1]

— McKinsey

While we have so far discussed Instacart from the perspective of a branded manufacturer, there is another serious stakeholder in this four-way marketplace: the retailers.

Retailers have more than a few reasons to be wary of Instacart. Our view is that many retailers are living on borrowed time, with their own ecommerce efforts lagging far behind Amazon and Instacart. But is the current reliance on Instacart to handle the notoriously challenging 'last mile' of retail fulfillment really all that bad?

. . .

If you're a branded manufacturer, don't immediately skip ahead. It's important to understand the pressures that your retail partners are under, and how the big changes they are facing have downstream impacts to you. In this chapter we'll explore retailers' mixed feelings toward Instacart, what retailers should consider as their next move, if Instacart will eventually become a retailer, and the implications of all this for the branded manufacturer.

Reasons for retailers to love Instacart

In a May 2019 report titled *Dissecting the Instacart Addiction*, Barclays Equity Research indeed categorized Instacart as an "addiction" for retailers, and that most retailers have no choice whether to work with Instacart in the near term. That's because Instacart solves several thorny challenges for retailers, like:

1. Providing the required technology, which many retailers are lagging behind on. Things like a working app, images, and integration with all the necessary phases from discovery, to picking, to delivery.
2. Facilitating same-day delivery windows. Last-mile delivery is hard, and very few operators have figured it out at scale. 'Route density' is a significant factor in making last-mile delivery profitable. Existing players like Instacart have already done the hard work to figure this out and optimize routes. They built their own maps

    infrastructure because Google Maps wasn't
    reliable for this purpose.

3. Using gig employees for picking and delivering: a
workaround for union operators who don't have
the ability to redeploy their existing employees.

Since the start of 2020, Instacart added more than 150 new retailers and welcomed more than 10,000 new store locations to the marketplace. So it's clear that not all retailers feel jittery about partnering with the service. Indeed, 2020 prompted more sign-ons than in the past — even Walmart started a pilot program with Instacart in 2020.

Avoiding the profit-sucking "last mile"

McKinsey's report, *Reviving the Grocery Industry: Six Imperatives* makes the argument that delivery costs are the biggest hurdle to profitability in online grocery.

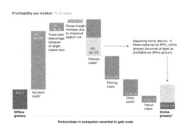

Image: McKinsey report, Reviving the grocery industry: six imperatives.[2]

One report from CommonSense Robotics found that grocers lose $5-15 on every manually picked order. Of course, the loss gets worse when the number of online orders increases.

And a study by Bain & Company found that in a home-delivery model, grocer margins can improve by 10% when a third party (i.e. Instacart) picks an order from a store, compared with the grocer's staff picking the order.[3]

Given the significant costs in both building the infrastructure (analytics, warehouse relocation, and automation) and the often-negative margin impact of fulfilling each order, it's easy to see why many retailers have passed the buck to Instacart. By outsourcing the last mile, retailers can preserve their margins, which is particularly important to grocery retailers who already operate on razor-thin profits.

> "Instacart is a low-cost option for retailers and I believe Sam's Club and Costco view Instacart as nothing more than a low-cost solution for a painful problem, picking and delivering groceries and other products in bulk to customers."

— Retail consultant Brittain Ladd in Forbes[4]

. . .

Nilam Ganenthiran, Instacart's President, told the Wall Street Journal that the company's services help grocers grow without spending years of work and capital investment to build infrastructure.[5] "We don't compete with retailers. We don't operate out of warehouses and haven't launched our own stores or mini-marts like other services that directly compete with grocers."

'Order density' is the other significant problem that grocers in particular are up against when designing their ecommerce solution. Low drop-density is the main reason for high delivery costs, according to McKinsey. This is where Instacart's business model shines: by aggregating across several retailers, it can achieve route density far more easily than a single retailer.

Skipping the learning curve

Instacart's own primary costs are the time it takes to shop for the groceries and to drive. In a lecture given by Jeremy Stanley, Instacart's former VP of Data Science, Instacart has been able to create profitable unit economics by focusing on these two areas. The company was able to drive down minutes-per-delivery by 40% through focusing on backend efficiency.[6]

This is a big advantage that retailers can leverage: skipping the learning curve that Instacart has already gone through.

· · ·

Instacart is where customers are already transacting

Some retailers have ventured into a click-and-collect model because it has a better margin profile than home delivery. (According to Bain, click-and-collect can be 4-10% more profitable, depending on how the order is picked.[7]) But this ignores the fact that most customers prefer a home delivery model. A Nielsen survey in 2018 found that of customers who shop online, 31% prefer curbside pickup, while 69% prefer home delivery.[8]

Customers want home delivery, and they are turning to apps like Instacart which reliably fulfil this need. The farther behind retailers get with meeting customer needs with a native solution, the more appealing it is to simply join the shopper where they are already transacting. Add to the fact that Instacart offers a plug-and-play solution, and it's easier to join Instacart than beat them.

Reasons for retailers to be wary of Instacart

Now that we understand why retailers have adopted Instacart so willingly, let's take a closer look at the challenges that the platform can create for retailers.

Losing the customer connection

When retailers become dependent on Instacart, they lose both their current and future direct relationship with the customer. The customer's contact information, product preferences, household information, and other data considered an important asset by most companies, is now collected and owned by Instacart.

The branding and customer shopping experience is shaped by Instacart's interface, too. If they can't find what they are looking for, it's easy for a customer to switch to a different retailer within the app. The customer is interacting with Instacart, not the retailer. As such, price becomes the key differentiator as the marketplace scales, not the relationship that a customer has with a retailer.

The report from Barclays Equity Research, *Dissecting the Instacart Addiction*, found that there were only two retailers where a customer would still go to that retailer to shop (if the retailer removed themselves from the app): Sprouts and Costco. If their chosen retailer suddenly disappeared from the Instacart platform, 43% of the customers surveyed said they would simply use a different retailer.

"As Instacart continues to develop stronger and stronger relationships with the customer, the customer starts thinking of Instacart as their provider, not the actual food retailer, and that becomes a very dangerous situation to be in, in my view, if you're a food retailer, especially a food retailer with limited differentiation." — Karen Short of Barclays Equity Research on the Digital Grocer podcast.[9]

.   .   .

The quandary of in-store shoppers

Instacart's in-store shoppers (those gig workers who pick items in-store for the end customer) have two key benefits for retailers: in a grocery store context they are more cost-effective than using a retailer's own staff,[10] and they also present an easy workaround for union-run retailers who cannot redeploy their existing employees to picking roles.

But retailers sometimes find their stores clogged with professional shoppers who are fighting for products alongside end customers. This creates a quandary for retailers — how to appropriately service both the in-store shoppers who need to find items and exit the store quickly, versus the end customer shopping for themselves, to whom you want to upsell convenience items?

Store layouts are currently optimized to increase basket sizes, not to facilitate fast shopping trips. In-store promotions, end-caps, and other shopper marketing techniques will become relics of the past, as they become more of a nuisance to professional shoppers navigating the aisles. With the balance shifting to professional shoppers, retailers can rely less on revenue streams from shopper marketing activities that are funded by branded manufacturers.

Margin erosion

According to the Barclays report, Instacart charges between 5-8% as a fee to retailers for every 'basket' or order placed on the app, similar to brands selling on Amazon's marketplace paying a 15% referral fee on the sale price to

Amazon. This means that retailers either look to recoup from customers, or cover the cost themselves.

In the latter case, if retailers do not pass this cost to customers in the form of a product markup on Instacart, they are losing 5-8% at the top line and much more at the bottom line.

Some retailers, like Costco and H-E-B,[11] do place a markup on their Instacart prices, getting customers to fund the difference. This makes Costco channel-agnostic, and keeps their margins in check. But per the point made earlier, with so many competing retailers on the platform, it's easy for a customer to price-compare and switch retailers, potentially making it a race to the bottom.

Instacart is also putting vendor allowances in jeopardy. Branded manufacturers are beginning to shift their promotions and advertising budgets online, so retailers could also see far less shopper marketing and vendor dollar revenue on the books.

The Barclays report looked at the vendor allowances of five of the top 50 largest US grocers and found that vendor allowances as a percentage of revenue ranged from 2-4% for smaller regional players to 7-9% for larger operators like Kroger and Safeway. (Vendor allowances or "vendor dollars" are rebates paid by manufacturers to retailers to offset their cost of promoting the manufacturer's products.

Examples include slotting fees, off-invoice deductions or markdowns, and incentive rebates.)

This is a highly profitable revenue stream for retailers, which could put considerable pressure on margins if manufacturers decide that Instacart should be the beneficiary of those dollars, given Instacart's place in the shopping journey. Barclays analysts say that inevitably, Instacart will siphon dollars away from these retailers, and this will result in profit margin erosion for retailers.

Will retailers build their own platform?

Ultimately, more revenue for Instacart is more revenue for the retailers that sell there. For retailers who do not have their own mature last-mile delivery play, they would otherwise be losing home-delivery sales right now. Larger retailers who are thinking strategically are likely to believe that they should eventually own the fulfillment process, or at least white-label it. But for many, that reality is far off.

Building an Instacart-equivalent solution is a mammoth task for even the biggest retailers. Kroger, the largest grocery retailer in the US, has looked to partnerships with technology companies to build its infrastructure. The retailer partnered with UK firm Ocado to build and operate its fulfillment and logistics infrastructure. The Kroger customer fulfilment centers (CFCs) use automation and artificial intelligence to service online grocery orders. As of November 2020, there were ten CFC sites identified for development in the US in partnership with Ocado.

. . .

To run its third party marketplace, Kroger partnered with software company Mirakl, a partnership announced in 2020. The CEO of Mirakl told Kiri in an interview that several more major grocery retailers will launch their own marketplace in 2021.

Retailers could leap-frog both their competitors and Instacart by investing in next-generation technology. While Instacart's current business model limits their efficiency to traditional store layouts and locations, retailers could flip the script through new concepts like dark stores and micro-fulfilment. A Westernacher report revealed manual workers pick on average 60-80 picks per hour; but an automated system can deliver at least 300 picks per hour.[12] Microfulfilment technology company AutoStore cites a 20-25% cost saving of an automated dark store compared to in-store picking. And companies that offer micro-fulfillment experience cost savings of 30-35% compared to in-store picking.[13]

Even with the hefty price tag, retailers could make that investment back, not just with anticipated retained market share and efficiency, but in hard dollars. Dean McElwee, Integrated Commercial Lead of E-Commerce for Europe at the Kellogg Company, says that every dollar that Instacart's advertising business gains is potentially a dollar that doesn't get spent at Walmart Media Services or Kroger Precision Marketing.

. . .

"Long-term ad profits will supplement ecommerce costs, so gaining as much of these dollars [as possible] will be a priority for the retailers themselves, leaving Instacart possibly exposed," said McElwee in a post on LinkedIn.[14]

Advertising revenue is one of the most profitable revenue sources that retailers could acquire. And it will be important to replace as they lose traditional shopper marketing dollars. Brand marketing teams need to place this budget somewhere, and they are increasingly seeing the value in retailer ad platforms. Research from the Digital Shelf Institute in 2020[15] found that both brands and retailers have measured up to a range of $7 to $11 spent in-store for every dollar spent online generated by retail media campaigns.

Retailers using Instacart as a test-bed

Here are some retailers who appear to be using Instacart as a means to an end:

- Walmart initiated a pilot with Instacart in late 2020, in four markets: Los Angeles, San Francisco, San Diego and Tulsa. At the same time, Walmart has been building its own digital offerings, including "Express Delivery" — a two-hour delivery service that it intends to roll out to 2,000 stores.
- Texan supermarket chain H-E-B has onboarded with Shipt, Instacart and some smaller delivery providers, ensuring they wouldn't become overly reliant on any one player. In 2018, H-E-

B acquired Favor, an on-demand delivery company.

- Target acquired Shipt to facilitate delivery of ecommerce orders from its stores. Against the current trend of building dedicated warehouses for fulfilment, Target has stated that most ecommerce fulfillment is done through their stores.

Some retailers might ultimately use a hybrid approach: their own solution for areas with high route-density, and Instacart for smaller cities where they cannot get the required scale for order density.

Will Instacart become a retailer itself?

As retailers regard Instacart as a potential "frenemy", it's worthwhile considering the likelihood of Instacart becoming a retailer itself. Chris Walton, a retail consultant said in a post for Forbes that digital entities like Instacart, DoorDash, and Amazon will continue to carve out more mindshare and provide consumers with even fewer reasons to visit physical stores.[16]

"If convenience is the barometer by which so many decisions are made and same-day delivery is also such an important part of that mental calculus, then how consumers think about their options and where they go physically and digitally will also start to change."

— Chris Walton, Forbes

This phenomenon is already happening in Europe with Delivery Hero, which relies heavily on its network of 148 'Dmarts', delivery-only supermarkets or warehouses located centrally and optimized for delivery, such that in some countries, goods are delivered in less than 15 minutes.[17]

Chris Cantino, the co-founder of CPG brand Schmidt's Naturals and co-founder of Color VC, thinks that Instacart could become a platform not just for major national brands and retailers, but for smaller DTC brands too. Instacart is a "demand aggregator," Cantino says, with in-built consumer awareness, trust, and same-day delivery. Cantino casts a vision whereby Instacart not only operates its own fulfillment centers, but creates its own private label brands and prepared meals, and sells excess capacity to DTC brands in a virtual pop-up format.

We can certainly see the potential in this model. Instacart has built the infrastructure to solve the notoriously difficult challenge of last-mile delivery, and they have earned the right to capitalize on that advantage for many years to come. But there is also an argument against this happening, with a solid case-study. Amazon started as a retailer, and dabbled in a 3P seller network. 15 years on, Amazon has found the 3P marketplace to outsell its 1P (retail) division on a Gross Merchandise Volume (GMV) basis. We also believe that Amazon's 3P business is overall more profitable than its 1P business. Instacart going from marketplace to retailer would be playing this out in reverse.

Instacart could also conceivably pivot to providing a white-label solution to retailers. In addition to actually being the shopping marketplace, they could sell the infrastructure to retailers, competing with the likes of Ocado and Mirakl. In fact, Instacart acquired a white-label platform for grocers in 2018, Toronto-based Unata. Unata's website now describes the company as an end-to-end digital grocery platform, with an optional Instacart integration, and counts Sprouts and Harmons as customers of its service.

The implication for brands

This exploration of the relationship between retailers and Instacart, now and in the future, leads us right back to the branded manufacturers. Whether or not there is a spectacular showdown between the two parties, brands should still consider how these events could impact them.

In the short term, there will be intense competition amongst retailers to differentiate on Instacart. This is likely to include pricing and selection:

- Pricing: Retailers will either take a hit to their own margins by being competitive with pricing on Instacart, or they will request funding from brands to make up the shortfall. As a brand, be prepared for these discussions, and consider what leverage you have in the situation. Are you spending on advertising for these SKUs? Show these promotional dollars (which ultimately benefit the retailer) in your negotiations. Could you give a retailer an exclusive on a subset of SKUs, allowing your retail customer to avoid downward pressure? Retailers may also expect brands to fund free delivery as a competitive advantage over another local grocery chain, or at least Instacart as a cudgel in trade negotiations with brands.

- Enhancing selection: Retailers might also look to expand the "long tail" of their assortment, delving into more niche products and also testing variations of top-sellers. This is a great opportunity for smaller brands to attract national distribution.

Looking out to the long term, when retailers do build (or buy) their own infrastructure outside of Instacart, brands will need to operate across an even more fractured set of online marketplaces. This means that advertising, operations management, and product content will all need to be managed individually or through the use of software. A brand that might actively work with three ecommerce platforms today (Amazon, Walmart, and Instacart, for example) might work with seven to ten in the future.

Retailers may also look to other mechanisms like private label brands as a way to differentiate and make up lost margin. This is already happening in full force across the grocery industry. Some players like Aldi and Lidl depend almost entirely on revenue from private label brands. Kroger's private label penetration is about 28%, while in the UK, Tesco offers more than 40% of all product under various private brands. The implication for brands is more competition from retailers themselves.

PART 5

PART V: WHO SHOULD BE INVOLVED IN EXECUTING MY INSTACART STRATEGY?

ONCE THE DECISION has been made to invest in Instacart, the next step is assembling a team to execute the plan. In full disclosure, we, the authors, operate an agency, Bobsled Marketing, that helps branded manufacturers to execute their marketplace strategy (including Instacart). In our work we encounter a broad spectrum of operating models that are successful both with and without agency involvement. While we will make the case for working with an agency and the use-cases that require it, we will also describe scenarios which could allow a manufacturer to operate with just an internal team.

Bring in experts vs. going it alone

Brands of all sizes and levels of sophistication seek the support of outside agency partners. This includes Fortune 500 companies right down to emerging brands. It can be a question of limited internal capacity or resourcing, or that the company needs to be assured that they are operating with best practices.

. . .

Jim Morgan, Head of Ecommerce & Digital Growth at Vita Coco, believes brands can benefit more from using a great external agency to manage Instacart campaigns, as the agency would have more experience and expertise as a result of working with different brands on the platform, and would therefore be better able to aggregate trends and implement best practices. Additional benefits Jim lists:

- Agencies may already manage your other ecommerce advertising channels, thereby providing you with simplicity (one consolidated view of your ecommerce media learnings and performance) and consistency (one cohesive strategy across multiple ecommerce platforms).
- Agencies might have a direct relationship with Instacart, making them more aware of new product developments and platform changes.

Many brands have their hands full already with Amazon. You may generate quicker wins with an outside agency solution to accelerate the strategy and then over time, consider things you can bring in house, or perhaps automate with technology.

Ingrid Milman Cordy, Head of Digital and Ecommerce at Nuun Hydration, says that companies that are equipped with internal PPC teams could handle Instacart internally since (right now) it is a fairly straightforward platform. She adds:

"PPC expertise is not something that is built in-house at a lot of companies, [so] layering this into the other PPC management that agencies offer is really important, especially if the Instacart program still resides on the sales team, which it does in a lot of places. That's even more reason for them to have an agency running it."

So what situations would imply that an agency is *not* required? We would suggest that a company could be self-reliant if the following things are true:

- Your company has been assigned an account manager at Instacart.
- An internal resource has extensive PPC experience on other ecommerce marketplaces (Amazon, Walmart, etc).
- This person has the bandwidth to learn and master a new sales channel, including initial set-up of new ad campaigns.
- This person (and/or their manager) has the ability to influence budget and supply chain decisions within other teams, primarily sales and brand marketing.
- This person is in frequent communication with peers at other companies of a similar size and industry who are willing to openly share experiences, best practices and benchmarks on a regular basis.

Appointing an owner

Regardless of whether you use an agency or handle the function internally, appointing ownership of the Instacart channel is critical. Melissa Burdick, Co-founder and President of ad-tech solution Pacvue, says that managing the channel is challenging for all stakeholders — Instacart, the ad-tech provider, and agencies — when there isn't a specific owner or champion.

Without an owner on the brand side, there is no dedicated person to conduct research, evaluate solutions and new opportunities, and to hold stakeholders accountable for results

Beyond that, there has to be someone to own the relationship with the agency and/or software solution, to provide direction on the overall strategy (e.g. a initiating a growth-oriented versus profitability-oriented bidding strategy), provide directions and parameters, approve budgets and in general manage the agency and/or software solution.

False Economies

Some brands understandably want to reduce the number of outside agencies and vendors that they work with. Indeed, some of the large agencies have built exclusivity clauses into their contracts which might limit a brand's ability to work with other agencies.

. . .

If the incumbent agency has Instacart experience, that's great, but we strongly advise against awarding the Instacart work to your incumbent agency if the primary criteria is to avoid managing another vendor.

In one instance, we worked on a consolidated strategic plan for one CPG brand's Instacart and Amazon Fresh channels. Despite us identifying a lot of efficiency issues and wasted opportunities in their execution to date (totalling in the hundreds of thousands of dollars in wasted ad spend and lost revenue per month), the brand decided to allow their existing shopper marketing agency to continue with the execution. Their rationale was to avoid appointing a specialist marketplace agency to reduce the number of agency vendors the brand worked with. The shopper marketing agency had no Instacart or Amazon Fresh experience, and a fairly limited track record of any form of PPC advertising results. In our view it's a false economy to save a few hours of administration and management in exchange for such significant lost opportunity and wasted ad spend.

Advertising optimization software

Third party software helps advertisers manage Instacart ads far more efficiently. Here are some of the ways that ad-tech software can help brands to better manage their Instacart ad spend:

- Campaign Automation. Rule-based optimization is a gamechanger for advertising in ecommerce, as it allows for extensive bid management and testing far beyond what manual effort would allow. Advertisers have the ability to set rules and conditions under which changes in bids, budgets or keywords will be executed automatically. Examples of automation include: If a keyword has more than five sales and ROI over $10 for a given period of time, increase bid by 20%. Another example would be if a keyword does not generate sales after 20 clicks, pause keyword. Other automation features can include AI optimization, campaign suggestions, and bulk campaign updates.

- Keyword Recommendations. Third party tools allow for faster and more efficient keyword research because users can input a main keyword and the tool provides recommendations for related search queries to that keyword.

- Customized Reporting. View results at an aggregate level, use tags to break down performance by product, and schedule regular reports. Customized reporting through an ad-tech software usually goes beyond what's available in the native Campaign manager dashboard.

- Budget Management — Manage with more control, including daypart bidding, out-of-budget tracking, and budget pacing. Budget management is very important for any PPC effort as brands usually operate with monthly budgets which are firmly set. If an ecommerce marketer does not pace the budget spending throughout the month they may find themselves with no budget to work with before the month ends. Dayparting is a powerful feature that allows the advertisers to set active days and time frames throughout the day to try to influence potential customers when they are most active. Dayparting is only available through third party software at the moment.

Another consideration when selecting an advertising technology solution is whether the solution effectively supports your other ecommerce platforms. While we strongly advocate for partnering with best-in-class software and solution providers, some software solutions can potentially also support your other ecommerce marketplaces. This allows for centralization of your advertising management with a single platform using a single log in, which is a benefit for the advertising professionals. This also allows for easier cross platform management, for example, transferring Amazon's profitable keywords to Instacart.

At our agency, Bobsled Marketing, we actively seek out leading software solutions for the channels that we support (Amazon, Instacart and Walmart). And while the process of changing software providers across 80+ client accounts is very painful, the overall gains in efficiency and better outcomes for our clients make the project of assessing, selecting, and onboarding with a new software solution worthwhile. In December 2020 we onboarded with Pacvue (and we have heard from co-founder Melissa Burdick several times in this book), as we found their solution to be best-in-class for both Amazon and Instacart.

Other solution providers

Throughout the book we have mentioned several solution providers that can support your Instacart growth strategy. Here's a recap of solution providers that we either have firsthand experience with, or have been recommended to us from brands we work with.

- MikMak: Helps brands to create 'multi-retailer shopping experience' by directing a brand's website or social traffic to various retailers including Instacart. e.l.f Cosmetics has worked with MikMak to allow visitors on the elfcosmetics.com website to select Instacart as a delivery option. Since e.l.f. is channel agnostic, they are thrilled with a solution that allows their customer to select the most convenient method of transacting for them. Website: www.mikmak.com

- Salsify: Commerce experience management platform for brands employing an omnichannel strategy. Brands selling across many online channels, and particularly those with extensive product catalogs, eventually require a sophisticated solution like Salsify, that serves as a single source of content truth, the syndication platform to all channels, inventory and order management for direct channels, and an analytics platform to optimize product detail page performance. At time of writing, Salsify also is the only solution that can syndicate product content to Instacart. Website: www.salsify.com

- Profitero: An ecommerce performance analytics platform helps brands to monitor product performance and benchmark against competitors across 600+ retailers, including Instacart. Website: www.profitero.com
- Pacvue: Advertising software solution for grocery and retail marketplaces, and our ad-tech solution of choice at Bobsled Marketing for clients advertising on Instacart, Walmart, and Amazon. Website: www.pacvue.com
- Bobsled Marketing: Our agency works with mid-sized consumer brands to optimize their Amazon, Walmart and Instacart sales channels. Depending on the needs of the brand, we can work on the strategy or execution side of the operations, brand protection, organic marketing, and advertising functions for these marketplaces. Website: www.bobsledmarketing.com

OVER THE PAST THREE YEARS, Kiri spent some time in Colombia, a country where digital personal shopping is surprisingly advanced. The key player in South America, Rappi, launched six years ago in Bogotá and is now active in nine South American markets.

Kiri shares her experience interacting with this next-generation shopping app:

"For expats and locals alike, Rappi is central to almost any delivery activity — whether ordering a weekly shop from a local supermarket, meal delivery from a restaurant or cloud kitchen, ordering items from external marketplaces like Amazon through "RappiMall", withdrawing cash from an ATM, peer-to-peer transactions like returning personal belongings to friends, and even requesting a 'Rappitendero' to walk your dog.

As a very frequent Rappi shopper I was quickly inducted into a frequent shopper program and able to use my bonus points as discounts on items. I also started receiving product samples from national brands."

In June 2020, Rappi launched a live streamed concert within the application and a Spotify-like music subscription service, consolidating its status as a "Super App".

Other Super Apps exist in Asian markets, such as WeChat, Grab and Gojek: apps that serve all-encompassing consumer needs around messaging, payments, news, social media, and shopping. While a good case has been made to assert that Super Apps are less likely to succeed in the US,[1] it is entirely likely that Instacart's future lies in extending beyond its current scope as a retail delivery app.

What's next for Instacart?

Chris Cantino, the co-founder of CPG brands Schmidt's Naturals and Color VC, sees a vision of the future where Instacart leverages its existing loyalty and traffic to operates its own fulfillment centers, creating its own private label brands and prepared meals, and selling excess capacity to DTC brands in a virtual pop-up format.

Instacart could also capitalize on the current app usage by bringing more social elements into its experience. Cantino sees Instacart rolling out features like shoppable live video streams from influencers, and a social graph showing interesting recent purchases that your friends have made. Creating a more immersive, social experience will undoubtedly open up opportunities for sponsored content from brands, display advertising, and opportunities to collaborate with influencers.

Instacart's shopping experience will move beyond just search-based queries, opening up far greater opportunities for brands to engage with customers. In a Q&A with Haixun Wang, Instacart's first VP of Algorithms, said that in the long term, the company's biggest challenge is to revolutionize the online shopping experience for its customers: [2]

"We need to go beyond the current "search, click, and ship" paradigm. Today, customers want to be informed, inspired, enlightened, and entertained. How do we do that? Well, certain technologies, such as conversational AI, augmented reality (AR), or combining ecommerce with social media will help, but more importantly, we need to rethink ecommerce with regard to its goal and scope."

In the nearer term, we believe that:

- Instacart will beef up its advertising and reporting capabilities quickly. Ad revenue is a highly profitable revenue stream for marketplaces, and now that Instacart has acquired the traffic and launched its version 1.0

advertising platform, improvements should rapidly follow. Unfortunately for us, we expect much of Chapter 7 ('A primer on Instacart advertising') and Chapter 9 ('How to measure success') to be out of date in less than a year. The upside for readers is that the changes should rapidly accelerate your ability to drive ad-generated sales quickly, efficiently, and with the numbers to make a great business case.

- Instacart will launch its own points-based loyalty programs, both for itself and for retailers. A job description for a Rewards and Loyalty Program Manager at Instacart says that the future role will "enable Retailers and Instacart to provide Coupons, Offers, Points, and other creative loyalty drivers to customers."[3]

- Larger retailers will seek to reduce their reliance on Instacart, building their own infrastructure. This will take time, but eventually brands will need to determine how to spread their performance and brand marketing budgets across a dozen or more retail media platforms. Instacart to help combat this with an Auto-ship or Subscribe & Save option for the every-week staples.

"Instacart does need more ways to make themselves even more sticky to both consumers and retailers with loyalty/points programs to keep both invested in Instacart success."

— Todd Hassenfelt, Simple Mills

Futureproofing: some thought experiments

Throughout this book, we have provided some forward-thinking views on what ecommerce could look like in the future. While we will undoubtedly get some of these wrong, it's never a waste of time to at least consider some predictions as thought experiments to ensure your strategy is future-proof.

Here are some of the predictions that we have shared throughout the book, and some thought experiments for each:

- Instacart's vantage point into household spending is significant, almost Amazon-like. Although the Instacart advertising platform is in its infancy now, it represents a huge, defensible growth opportunity for Instacart and is likely to be developed rapidly. How will Instacart fit into your brands' advertising funnel? Does Instacart actually hit multiple sections of your purchase journey?
- Most mid-sized brands already consider themselves "omnichannel", but how omni are you prepared to get? If retailers start building their own delivery capabilities in order to regain control over the customer experience, brands will need to interact with many more ecommerce channels. How will you scale your

operations efforts (inventory forecasting, content, catalog management) and advertising budgets across a dozen retailer platforms?

- What changes must be made to your attribution model to account for Instacart spend and retail trade spend to measure incremental revenue? This endeavor is complicated by the lack of retailer-level data from Instacart.

- Most brands have already had their forecasting models challenged by the shift to ecommerce. If you ramp up advertising and promotions on Instacart, how does your forecasting model need to change to account for increased demand?

- Like Amazon, so much of Instacart performance is interconnected with other business factors. You need your retail spend synced up with your marketing content, synced up with your supply chain. Looking at your organizational structure and accountabilities, what might need to change to ensure everyone is pulling in the same direction?

- Retailers may look to make up lost margins (from erosion in vendor allowances, lost shopper marketing spend, and the economics of facilitating home delivery or click and collect) with developing more private label brands. As a brand, what is your strategy to deal with competition from private labels?

- Profitability across ecommerce channels is a challenge that many traditional brands face, especially those in the CPG category. If retailer partners look to pass some of the cost of servicing Instacart back to brands, how will that affect you? How much margin do you have left to play with across your assortment?

- There is a fractious relationship between some retailers and Instacart (see Chapter 10). Brands are fully reliant on retailers to cooperate with Instacart, in order to have an inventory position on the marketplace. How cooperative are your primary retailers with Instacart? What is their long-term view on the partnership? How can you mitigate the risk of key retailer accounts inadvertently causing you to go dark on Instacart?

- What has your company earmarked as its "innovation" budget? (We find a lot of companies allocate 10% of their baseline budget here.) How does Instacart's current and future marketing capabilities fit into your marketing budget — innovation or core?

What to do now

We have covered a lot of ground in this book, and it can be overwhelming to know where to start. This is not an exhaustive list by any means, but if you're just getting started (or have skipped around in the content in the book), here's a recap of what we recommend you do.

Assortment availability:

1. Is your brand already on Instacart? It may very well be without you knowing it. Search for your brand name or products on Instacart using several different zip codes.

2. If your brand is not already sold on Instacart, contact your major retail partners. Retailers are feeding Instacart with data, adding details for products that are being sold there.

3. If your brands' products are being sold on Instacart but you don't see all of them, identify the UPCs that are missing and get in touch with Instacart. They are usually just as eager to have your full assortment available as you are.

4. If you need to update content on your product listings utilize a content syndication tool like Salsify to make sure your product feed content is unified across platforms. A digital shelf analytics tool like Profitero can then close the loop and make sure the expected content is actually showing up everyday.

Demand generation:

1. Before you get started with Featured Products: get feedback from the sales team within your company about current and expected inventory availability.

2. Invest in Featured Products as early as possible. There is undoubtedly a first-mover advantage at the moment.

3. Get internal agreement on overall advertising priorities: are you wanting to aggressively grow market share, or maintain a specific level of profitability? Each priority will dictate a different bidding and campaign strategy.

4. Rely on lessons learned from other ecommerce platforms, Amazon and Walmart in particular. Start with converting search terms from Amazon, utilize competing SKUs as guides towards discovering your products value adds over competitor products.

5. Select an ad-tech partner that will meet your current needs around automating bidding, building campaigns, generating reports etc. Make sure your chosen ad-tech partner is committed to investing future development in Instacart capabilities.

6. Consider the keywords that you'll be bidding on through the full customer purchase journey: conquesting and defending your brand search terms, acquiring market share from competitors, driving awareness of your product, driving awareness of the solution.

7. Combine Featured Products and coupons to improve click through rates.

8. Measure your share of search on Instacart against competitors and to see who is conquesting your brand most frequently.

9. Be sure to select as many ad slots as Instacart offers (currently the number is three) so that competitors cannot sneak in.

10. Think about your own grocery list: do you

choose by brand or by product type? Keep that in mind when advertising.

11. Consider working with an agency like Bobsled Marketing to save time, stay up-to-date on all new advertising releases, and work on customizable solutions directly with Instacart.

Strategy:

1. Determine your current and (if necessary) ideal future organization chart. Who's accountable for results, and who's responsible for executing the plan? In Chapter 8 we discuss the pros and cons of having Instacart managed within various internal departments.

2. Assign an Instacart 'owner' who will manage the various solution providers and report outcomes.

3. Determine an advertising budget for initiating your Instacart efforts. Identify a timeframe to reassign this from "innovation" budget to "business as usual" budget.

4. Determine your criteria for success. KPIs should align with business needs but also be within the scope of what is possible to measure right now. That takes retailer-level sales off the table.

Sharpen the saw:

Don't stop your learning journey here! As we've said, Instacart is changing quickly and it's key to stay updated.

1. Subscribe to our Instacart newsletter at Bobsled Marketing; we will be sharing updates to our research along the way. (www.bobsledmarketing.com)

2. Subscribe to Kiri's podcast, Ecommerce Braintrust, which covers ecommerce marketplace topics. You can stream episodes from www.ecommercebraintrust.com or search for "Ecommerce Braintrust" in Apple podcasts or your favorite podcast app.

3. Join a peer learning network. Immense value can be found through connecting with peers and sharing best practices together. Some groups that might be suitable include the Digital Shelf Institute (www.digitalshelfinstitute.org), Firstmovr (www.firstmovr.com/), BWG Connect (www.bwgstrategy.com), and various Facebook and LinkedIn groups dedicated to peer networking.

4. Connect with Stefan and Kiri on LinkedIn; we are both avid content creators and curators (linkedin.com/in/kiri-masters and linkedin.com/in/jordevstefan).

5. Check out Kiri's 2019 book, *Amazon for CMOs*, for a similar executive-level discussion on the Amazon marketplace. It was recently recognized as one of the top 20 retail books of all time by Book Authority.

Finally, if you have gotten value from this book, it would mean so much to us if you could provide a rating or review on Amazon. Your review will help your peers to discover this book so we can continue to figure out this new platform together.

INTRODUCTION

1. "95 Best Retail Books of All Time," Bookauthority, accessed January, 15, 2021, https://bookauthority.org/books/best-retail-books

1. HOW THE INSTACART MARKETPLACE WORKS

1. Chris Powell, "How a wave of delivery startups are remaking grocery shopping," Canadian Business, September 15, 2015, https://www.-canadianbusiness.com/innovation/how-a-wave-of-delivery-startups-are-remaking-grocery-shopping/
2. Karen Short, Sylvain Perrier, Mark Fairhurst, "Interview with Barclays on "Dissecting the Instacart Addiction"," July 8, 2019, https://www.mercatus.com/blog/resources/podcasts/interview-with-barclays-on-dissecting-the-instacart-addiction/
3. Sarah Perez, "COVID-19 pandemic accelerated shift to e-commerce by 5 years, new report says," TechCrunch, August 24, 2020, https://techcrunch.com/2020/08/24/covid-19-pandemic-accelerated-shift-to-e-commerce-by-5-years-new-report-says/
4. "Percentage of paid units sold by third-party sellers on Amazon platform as of 3rd quarter 2020," Statista, accessed January 15, 2021, https://www.statista.com/statistics/259782/third-party-seller-share-of-amazon-platform/

2. HOW INSTACART COMPARES TO OTHER ONLINE MARKETPLACES

1. Bobsled Analysis. Shopper Frequency data from Cowen and Company US Internet Consumer Tracker, Mid-August 2020
2. Kiri Masters, "Bezos Admits To Serious Issues For Retail Brands In Antitrust Inquiry. What Will Change?," Forbes, July 30, 2020, https://www.forbes.com/sites/kirimasters/2020/07/30/bezos-admits-

to-serious-issues-for-retail-brands-in-antitrust-inquiry-what-will-
change/?sh=55d959207a84

3. INSTACART TODAY

1. Gina Acosta, "The Predictable Rise of Instacart," Progressive grocer, October 9, 2020, https://progressivegrocer.com/predictable-rise-instacart

2. Kate Gessner, "Instacart dominates delivery, while top grocers see little shift in market share" — Second Measure, August 13, 2020, https://secondmeasure.com/datapoints/grocery-spending-delivery-trends/

4. THE CASE FOR INSTACART IN THE FUTURE

1. "eGrocery's New Reality: The Pandemic's Lasting Impact on U.S. Grocery Shopping Behavior," Mercatus, September 2020, https://info.mercatus.com/egrocery-shopper-behavior-report?utm_source=ketner&utm_medium=media&utm_campaign=fy21-q3-shopper-survey-report-ketner-press-release

2. Justin Manly, Jimmy Royston, and Morgan Sonntag, "CPG Companies Face an E-Commerce Tsunami", Boston Consulting Group, July 9, 2020, https://www.bcg.com/publications/2020/cpg-companies-face-increased-e-commerce

3. Andrew Lipsman, 10 Key Digital Trends for 2021, Insider Intelligence Inc.

4. Bank of America "COVID-19 Investment Implications Series: From brick to click & everything between ", 2020

5. Tom Ryan, "Has the pandemic proven Instacart's business model?," Retail Wire, June 19, 2020, https://retailwire.com/discussion/has-the-pandemic-proven-instacarts-business-model/

6. Jaewon Kang, "Instacart Looked Like a Savior. Now Stores Aren't So Sure.," The Wall Street Journal, December 28, 2020, https://www.wsj.com/articles/instacart-looked-like-a-savior-now-stores-arent-so-sure-11609151401?mod=searchresults_pos3&page=1

7. Kang, "Instacart Looked Like a Savior. Now Stores Aren't So Sure,"

8. www.dumpling.us

5. INSTACART OPERATIONS FUNDAMENTALS

1. Tom Goodwin, *The Battle is for the customer interface*, Techcrunch, March 4, 2015, https://techcrunch.com/2015/03/03/in-the-age-of-disintermediation-the-battle-is-all-for-the-customer-interface/
2. Instacart Advertising Guide for Alcohol Brands by PacVue, page 1, accessed September 21, 2020, https://www.pacvue.com/discover/reports/advertising-guide-alcohol-on-instacart?utm_campaign=Advertising%20Guide%3A%20Alcohol%20on%20Instacart&utm_source=bobsledbook

7. A PRIMER ON INSTACART PERFORMANCE ADVERTISING

1. Kyle Wiggers, "How Instacart remade its systems to handle a 500% jump in order volume," Venture Beat, May 21, 2020, https://venturebeat.com/2020/05/21/how-instacart-remade-its-systems-to-handle-a-500-jump-in-order-volume/
2. "Top 100 Retailers 2020 List," National Retail Federation, accessed January 15, 2020, https://nrf.com/resources/top-retailers/top-100-retailers/top-100-retailers-2020-list
3. Lauren Johnson, "Instacart just raised $200 million to expand its advertising business — here's a look inside its strategy", Business Insider, December 14, 2020, https://www.businessinsider.com/inside-instacarts-advertising-business-2020-2020-10?r=AU&IR=T ,
4. Director, Data Science (ADS), Instacart- Careers, accessed December 6, 2020
   https://instacart.careers/job/?id=2240747
5. "Building an Ad Engine for Grocery," Tech-at-instacart, September 29, 2020,
   https://tech.instacart.com/building-an-ad-engine-for-grocery-8d6bb1753831

9. HOW TO MEASURE SUCCESS

1. Lauren Johnson, "Instacart just raised $200 million to expand its advertising business — here's a look inside its strategy," Business Insider, December 14, 2020, https://www.businessinsider.com/inside-instacarts-advertising-business-2020-2020-10?r=AU&IR=T
2. Tom Crosthwaite,"CommerceLive 2020 CPG & Grocery Recap," Bobsled Marketing, May 21,2020, https://blog.bobsledmarketing.com/blog/commercelive-2020-cpg-grocery-recap

3. Kiri Masters, "The Surprising Impact Of Retail Advertising Investment For Brands", Forbes, December 17, 2020, https://www.forbes.com/sites/kirimasters/2020/12/17/the-surprising-impact-of-retail-advertising-investment-for-brands/?sh=26edbeeb3cea

10. THE RETAILER CONNECTION

1. Dymfke Kuijpers, Virginia Simmons, and Jasper van Wamelen, "Reviving grocery retail: Six imperatives," McKinsey&Company, December 3, 2018, https://www.mckinsey.com/industries/retail/our-insights/reviving-grocery-retail-six-imperatives
2. Kuijpers,Simmons,and van Wamelen, "Reviving grocery retail: Six imperatives,"
3. Marc-André Kamel, Joëlle de Montgolfier, Stephen Caine, et al., "How to Ramp Up Online Grocery—without Breaking the Bank," Bain & Company, July 200, 2020, https://www.bain.com/insights/how-to-ramp-up-online-grocery-without-breaking-the-bank/
4. Brittain Ladd, "Killing Instacart: Why The High-Flying Company Is At Risk Of Crashing To The Ground," Forbes, February 11, 2019, https://www.forbes.com/sites/brittainladd/2019/02/11/killing-instacart-why-the-company-is-at-risk-of-crashing-to-the-ground/?sh=5de60bbf36e8
5. Jaewon Kang, "Instacart Looked Like a Savior. Now Stores Aren't So Sure.,' The Wall Street Journal, December 28, 2020, https://www.wsj.com/articles/instacart-looked-like-a-savior-now-stores-arent-so-sure-11609151401?mod=searchresults_pos3&page=1
6. Jeremy Stanley, "Data Science at Instacart: Making On-Demand Profitable," Domino, March 20, 2017, https://blog.dominodatalab.com/data-science-instacart/
7. Kamel, de Montgolfier,Caine,et al., "How to Ramp Up Online Grocery—without Breaking the Bank,"
8. Jessica Dumont, "Study: Shoppers prefer grocery delivery over in-store pickup," Grocery Dive, January 30, 2019, https://www.grocerydive.com/news/study-shoppers-prefer-grocery-delivery-over-in-store-pickup/547173/
9. The Digital Grocer podcast, "Barclays Investment Bank's Karen Short on Dissecting the Instacart Addiction", August 28, 2020, 22:17, https://digitalgrocer.com/podcasts/barclays-investment-banks-karen-short-on-dissecting-the-instacart-addiction-grocery-podcast-s2-e3/
10. Kamel, de Montgolfier,Caine,et al., "How to Ramp Up Online Grocery—without Breaking the Bank,"
11. Jaewon Kang, "Instacart Looked Like a Savior. Now Stores Aren't So Sure.,' The Wall Street Journal, December 28, 2020,

https://www.wsj.com/articles/instacart-looked-like-a-savior-now-stores-arent-so-sure-11609151401?mod=searchresults_pos3&page=1

12. Marco Trottmann, Sam Zhang "The trend towards warehouse automation," Westernacher, 2017, https://westernacher-consulting.com/wp-content/uploads/2017/11/Whitepaper_Trend_to_Automation_FINAL_s.pdf

13. "Online Grocery Order Fulfillment Cost Comparison," MWPVL, accessed January 28, 2021, https://mwpvl.com/html/online_grocery_order_fulfillment_cost_comparison.html

14. Dean McElwee, Linkedin, accessed January, 7, 2021, https://www.linkedin.com/posts/activity-6734381518870888448-4IYf

15. "The Full Revenue Impact of Retailer Ad Platforms," Digital Shelf Institute, accessed January 28, 2021, https://www.digitalshelfinstitute.org/the-full-revenue-impact-of-retailer-ad-platforms

16. Chris Walton, "The 5 Most Important Retail Events Of 2020 Had Nothing To Do With Covid-19," Forbes, December 9, 2020, https://www.forbes.com/sites/christopherwalton/2020/12/09/the-5-most-important-retail-events-of-2020-actually-had-almost-nothing-to-do-with-covid-19

17. Chloe Gamache, "The key to successfully launching and running Dmarts," Delivery Hero, July, 29, 2020, https://www.deliveryhero.com/blog/the-key-to-successfully-launching-and-running-dmarts/

12. WHAT'S NEXT?

1. Christopher Chen, "Why China's "super-apps" will never succeed in the US," Prototype.io, May 20, 2020, https://blog.prototypr.io/why-chinas-super-apps-will-never-succeed-in-the-us-64c686c8c5d6

2. "A small engineering team with a big impact," Tech At Instacart blog, Jul 15, 2020, https://tech.instacart.com/a-small-engineering-team-with-a-big-impact-40184c40d7e

3. "Senior Product Manager, Retail," Instacart- Careers, accessed December 18, 2020, https://instacart.careers/job/?id=2379987

CPSIA information can be obtained
at www.ICGtesting.com
Printed in the USA
BVHW071209180321
602885BV00007B/803